SHAKESPEARE'S LOVE POETRY

SHAKESPEARE'S LOVE POETRY

selected by **Thomas Blaikie**

MACMILLAN LONDON

First published 1983 by
PAPERMAC
a division of Macmillan Publishers Limited
4 Little Essex Street London WC2R 3LF
and Basingstoke

Associated companies in Auckland, Dallas, Delhi, Dublin,
Hong Kong, Johannesburg, Lagos, Manzini, Melbourne, Nairobi,
New York, Singapore, Tokyo, Washington and Zaria

ISBN 0 333 35989 5

Printed in Hong Kong

Acknowledgements
The Publishers are grateful to Houghton Mifflin Inc for permission to
use the extract from *The Two Noble Kinsmen* from the Riverside Edition of
The Complete Works of Shakespeare and to William Collins Limited for kind
permission to use the Alexander Text for the rest of this selection.

Contents

The
Sonnets

TO. THE. ONLIE. BEGETTER. OF.
THESE. INSUING. SONNETS.
MR. W. H. ALL. HAPPINESSE.
AND. THAT. ETERNITIE.
PROMISED.
BY.
OUR. EVER-LIVING. POET.
WISHETH.
THE. WELL-WISHING.
ADVENTURER. IN.
SETTING.
FORTH.

T. T.

❧ 1 ❧

From fairest creatures we desire increase,
That thereby beauty's rose might never die,
But as the riper should by time decrease,
His tender heir might bear his memory;
But thou, contracted to thine own bright eyes,
Feed'st thy light's flame with self-substantial fuel,
Making a famine where abundance lies,
Thyself thy foe, to thy sweet self too cruel.
Thou that art now the world's fresh ornament
And only herald to the gaudy spring,
Within thine own bud buriest thy content,
And, tender churl, mak'st waste in niggarding.
Pity the world, or else this glutton be,
To eat the world's due, by the grave and thee.

2

When forty winters shall besiege thy brow,
And dig deep trenches in thy beauty's field,
Thy youth's proud livery, so gaz'd on now,
Will be a tatter'd weed of small worth held.
Then being ask'd where all thy beauty lies,
Where all the treasure of thy lusty days,
To say within thine own deep-sunken eyes
Were an all-eating shame and thriftless praise.
How much more praise deserv'd thy beauty's use,
If thou couldst answer 'This fair child of mine
Shall sum my count, and make my old excuse'
Proving his beauty by succession thine!
This were to be new made when thou art old,
And see thy blood warm when thou feel'st it cold.

❦ 3 ❦

Look in thy glass, and tell the face thou viewest
Now is the time that face should form another;
Whose fresh repair if now thou not renewest,
Thou dost beguile the world, unbless some mother.
For where is she so fair whose unear'd womb
Disdains the tillage of thy husbandry?
Or who is he so fond will be the tomb
Of his self-love, to stop posterity?
Thou art thy mother's glass, and she in thee
Calls back the lovely April of her prime;
So thou through windows of thine age shalt see,
Despite of wrinkles, this thy golden time.
But if thou live rememb'red not to be,
Die single, and thine image dies with thee.

✤ 4 ✤

Unthrifty loveliness, why dost thou spend
Upon thyself thy beauty's legacy?
Nature's bequest gives nothing, but doth lend,
And, being frank, she lends to those are free.
Then, beauteous niggard, why dost thou abuse
The bounteous largess given thee to give?
Profitless usurer, why dost thou use
So great a sum of sums, yet canst not live?
For having traffic with thyself alone,
Thou of thyself thy sweet self dost deceive.
Then how when nature calls thee to be gone,
What acceptable audit canst thou leave?
Thy unus'd beauty must be tomb'd with thee,
Which, used, lives th' executor to be.

❧ 5 ❧

Those hours that with gentle work did frame
The lovely gaze where every eye doth dwell
Will play the tyrants to the very same,
And that unfair which fairly doth excel;
For never-resting time leads summer on
To hideous winter, and confounds him there;
Sap check'd with frost and lusty leaves quite gone,
Beauty o'ersnow'd, and bareness every where.
Then, were not summer's distillation left
A liquid prisoner pent in walls of glass,
Beauty's effect with beauty were bereft,
Nor it, nor no remembrance what it was;
But flowers distill'd, though they with winter meet,
Leese but their show: their substance still lives sweet.

freezing

❧ 6 ❧

Then let not winter's ragged hand deface
In thee thy summer ere thou be distill'd;
Make sweet some vial; treasure thou some place
With beauty's treasure ere it be self-kill'd.
That use is not forbidden usury
Which happies those that pay the willing loan—
That's for thyself to breed an other thee,
Or ten times happier, be it ten for one;
Ten times thy self were happier than thou art,
If ten of thine ten times refigur'd thee.
Then what could Death do if thou shouldst depart,
Leaving thee living in posterity?
Be not self-will'd, for thou art much too fair
To be death's conquest and make worms thine heir.

❧ 7 ❧

Lo, in the orient when the gracious light
Lifts up his burning head, each under eye
Doth homage to his new-appearing sight,
Serving with looks his sacred majesty;
And having climb'd the steep-up heavenly hill,
Resembling strong youth in his middle age,
Yet mortal looks adore his beauty still,
Attending on his golden pilgrimage;
But when from highmost pitch, with weary car,
Like feeble age he reeleth from the day,
The eyes, 'fore duteous, now converted are
From his low tract and look another way;
So thou, thyself outgoing in thy noon,
Unlook'd on diest, unless thou get a son.

❦ 8 ❧

Music to hear, why hear'st thou music sadly?
Sweets with sweets war not, joy delights in joy.
Why lov'st thou that which thou receiv'st not gladly,
Or else receiv'st with pleasure thine annoy?
If the true concord of well-tuned sounds,
By unions married, do offend thine ear,
They do but sweetly chide thee, who confounds
In singleness the parts that thou shouldst bear.
Mark how one string, sweet husband to another,
Strikes each in each by mutual ordering;
Resembling sire, and child, and happy mother,
Who, all in one, one pleasing note do sing;
Whose speechless song, being many, seeming one,
Sings this to thee: 'Thou single wilt prove none'.

🏵 9 🏵

Is it for fear to wet a widow's eye
That thou consum'st thyself in single life?
Ah! if thou issueless shalt hap to die,
The world will wail thee like a makeless wife:
The world will be thy widow, and still weep
That thou no form of thee hast left behind,
When every private widow well may keep,
By children's eyes, her husband's shape in mind.
Look what an unthrift in the world doth spend
Shifts but his place, for still the world enjoys it;
But beauty's waste hath in the world an end,
And kept unus'd, the user so destroys it.
No love toward others in that bosom sits
That on himself such murd'rous shame commits.

❧ 10 ❧

For shame! deny that thou bear'st love to any,
Who for thy self art so unprovident.
Grant, if thou wilt, thou art belov'd of many,
But that thou none lov'st is most evident;
For thou art so possess'd with murd'rous hate
That 'gainst thyself thou stick'st not to conspire,
Seeking that beauteous roof to ruinate
Which to repair should be thy chief desire.
O, change thy thought, that I may change my mind!
Shall hate be fairer lodg'd than gentle love?
Be, as thy presence is, gracious and kind,
Or to thy self at least kind-hearted prove;
Make thee an other self for love of me,
That beauty still may live in thine or thee.

❧ 11 ❧

As fast as thou shalt wane, so fast thou grow'st
In one of thine, from that which thou departest;
And that fresh blood which youngly thou bestow'st
Thou mayst call thine when thou from youth convertest.
Herein lives wisdom, beauty, and increase;
Without this folly, age, and cold decay.
If all were minded so, the times should cease,
And threescore year would make the world away.
Let those whom Nature hath not made for store,
Harsh, featureless, and rude, barrenly perish.
Look whom she best endow'd she gave the more;
Which bounteous gift thou shouldst in bounty cherish;
She carv'd thee for her seal, and meant thereby
Thou shouldst print more, not let that copy die.

✇ 12 ✇

When I do count the clock that tells the time,
And see the brave day sunk in hideous night;
When I behold the violet past prime,
And sable curls all silver'd o'er with white;
When lofty trees I see barren of leaves,
Which erst from heat did canopy the herd,
And summer's green all girded up in sheaves
Borne on the bier with white and bristly beard;
Then of thy beauty do I question make
That thou among the wastes of time must go,
Since sweets and beauties do themselves forsake,
And die as fast as they see others grow;
And nothing 'gainst Time's scythe can make defence
Save breed, to brave him when he takes thee hence.

13

O that you were yourself! But, love, you are
No longer yours than you your self here live.
Against this coming end you should prepare,
And your sweet semblance to some other give.
So should that beauty which you hold in lease
Find no determination; then you were
Your self again, after your self's decease,
When your sweet issue your sweet form should bear.
Who lets so fair a house fall to decay,
Which husbandry in honour might uphold
Against the stormy gusts of winter's day
And barren rage of death's eternal cold?
O, none but unthrifts! Dear my love, you know
You had a father: let your son say so.

❧ 14 ❧

Not from the stars do I my judgment pluck,
And yet methinks I have astronomy;
But not to tell of good or evil luck,
Of plagues, of dearths, or seasons' quality;
Nor can I fortune to brief minutes tell,
Pointing to each his thunder, rain, and wind,
Or say with princes if it shall go well
By oft predict that I in heaven find;
But from thine eyes my knowledge I derive,
And, constant stars, in them I read such art
As truth and beauty shall together thrive,
If from thy self to store thou wouldst convert.
Or else of thee this I prognosticate:
Thy end is truth's and beauty's doom and date.

No upside

✥ 15 ✥

When I consider every thing that grows
Holds in perfection but a little moment,
That this huge stage presenteth nought but shows
Whereon the stars in secret influence comment;
When I perceive that men as plants increase,
Cheered and check'd even by the self-same sky,
Vaunt in their youthful sap, at height decrease,
And wear their brave state out of memory;
Then the conceit of this inconstant stay
Sets you most rich in youth before my sight,
Where wasteful Time debateth with Decay
To change your day of youth to sullied night;
And all in war with Time for love of you,
As he takes from you, I engraft you new.

not plea

17

❧ 16 ❧

But wherefore do not you a mightier way
Make war upon this bloody tyrant Time?
And fortify your self in your decay
With means more blessed than my barren rhyme?
Now stand you on the top of happy hours,
And many maiden gardens, yet unset,
With virtuous wish would bear your living flowers,
Much liker than your painted counterfeit;
So should the lines of life that life repair,
Which this, Time's pencil or my pupil pen,
Neither in inward worth, nor outward fair,
Can make you live your self in eyes of men.
To give away your self keeps your self still;
And you must live, drawn by your own sweet skill.

✿ 17 ✿

Who will believe my verse in time to come,
If it were fill'd with your most high deserts?
Though yet, heaven knows, it is but as a tomb
Which hides your life and shows not half your parts.
If I could write the beauty of your eyes
And in fresh numbers number all your graces,
The age to come would say 'This poet lies;
Such heavenly touches ne'er touch'd earthly faces'.
So should my papers, yellowed with their age,
Be scorn'd, like old men of less truth than tongue;
And your true rights be term'd a poet's rage,
And stretched metre of an antique song.
But were some child of yours alive that time,
You should live twice—in it, and in my rhyme.

🕸 18 🕸

Shall I compare thee to a summer's day?
Thou art more lovely and more temperate.
Rough winds do shake the darling buds of May,
And summer's lease hath all too short a date:
Sometime too hot the eye of heaven shines,
And often is his gold complexion dimm'd;
And every fair from fair some time declines,
By chance, or nature's changing course, untrimm'd;
But thy eternal summer shall not fade
Nor lose possession of that fair thou ow'st;
Nor shall Death brag thou wand'rest in his shade,
When in eternal lines to time thou grow'st.
So long as men can breathe or eyes can see,
So long lives this, and this gives life to thee.

✿ 19 ✿

Devouring Time, blunt thou the lion's paws,
And make the earth devour her own sweet brood;
Pluck the keen teeth from the fierce tiger's jaws,
And burn the long-liv'd phœnix in her blood;
Make glad and sorry seasons as thou fleet'st,
And do whate'er thou wilt, swift-footed Time,
To the wide world and all her fading sweets;
But I forbid thee one most heinous crime:
O, carve not with thy hours my love's fair brow,
Nor draw no lines there with thine antique pen;
Him in thy course untainted do allow
For beauty's pattern to succeeding men.
Yet, do thy worst, old Time. Despite thy wrong,
My love shall in my verse ever live young.

❦ 20 ❦

A woman's face, with Nature's own hand painted,
Hast thou, the Master Mistress of my passion;
A woman's gentle heart, but not acquainted
With shifting change, as is false woman's fashion;
An eye more bright than theirs, less false in rolling,
Gilding the object whereupon it gazeth;
A man in hue all hues in his controlling,
Which steals men's eyes and women's souls amazeth.
And for a woman wert thou first created;
Till Nature, as she wrought thee, fell a-doting,
And by addition me of thee defeated
By adding one thing to my purpose nothing.
But since she prick'd thee out for women's pleasure,
Mine be thy love, and thy love's use their treasure.

✣ 21 ✣

So is it not with me as with that Muse,
Stirr'd by a painted beauty to his verse;
Who heaven itself for ornament doth use,
And every fair with his fair doth rehearse,
Making a couplement of proud compare
With sun and moon, with earth and sea's rich gems,
With April's first-born flowers, and all things rare
That heaven's air in this huge rondure hems.
O, let me, true in love, but truly write,
And then believe me, my love is as fair
As any mother's child, though not so bright
As those gold candles fix'd in heaven's air.
Let them say more that like of hearsay well:
I will not praise that purpose not to sell.

❧ 22 ❧

My glass shall not persuade me I am old
So long as youth and thou are of one date;
But when in thee time's furrows I behold,
Then look I death my days should expiate.
For all that beauty that doth cover thee
Is but the seemly raiment of my heart,
Which in thy breast doth live, as thine in me;
How can I then be elder than thou art?
O, therefore, love, be of thyself so wary,
As I not for myself but for thee will;
Bearing thy heart, which I will keep so chary
As tender nurse her babe from faring ill.
Presume not on thy heart when mine is slain;
Thou gav'st me thine, not to give back again.

❦ 23 ❦

As an unperfect actor on the stage
Who with his fear is put besides his part,
Or some fierce thing replete with too much rage,
Whose strength's abundance weakens his own heart;
So I, for fear of trust, forget to say
The perfect ceremony of love's rite,
And in mine own love's strength seem to decay,
O'ercharg'd with burthen of mine own love's might.
O, let my looks be then the eloquence
And dumb presagers of my speaking breast;
Who plead for love, and look for recompense,
More than that tongue that more hath more express'd.
O, learn to read what silent love hath writ!
To hear with eyes belongs to love's fine wit.

❧ 24 ❧

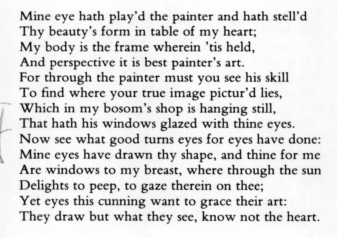

Mine eye hath play'd the painter and hath stell'd
Thy beauty's form in table of my heart;
My body is the frame wherein 'tis held,
And perspective it is best painter's art.
For through the painter must you see his skill
To find where your true image pictur'd lies,
Which in my bosom's shop is hanging still,
That hath his windows glazed with thine eyes.
Now see what good turns eyes for eyes have done:
Mine eyes have drawn thy shape, and thine for me
Are windows to my breast, where through the sun
Delights to peep, to gaze therein on thee;
Yet eyes this cunning want to grace their art:
They draw but what they see, know not the heart.

25

Let those who are in favour with their stars
Of public honour and proud titles boast,
Whilst I, whom fortune of such triumph bars,
Unlook'd for joy in that I honour most.
Great princes' favourites their fair leaves spread
But as the marigold at the sun's eye;
And in themselves their pride lies buried,
For at a frown they in their glory die.
The painful warrior famoused for fight,
After a thousand victories once foil'd,
Is from the book of honour razed quite,
And all the rest forgot for which he toil'd.
Then happy I, that love and am beloved
Where I may not remove nor be removed.

✺ 26 ✺

Lord of my love, to whom in vassalage
Thy merit hath my duty strongly knit,
To thee I send this written embassage,
To witness duty, not to show my wit;
Duty so great, which wit so poor as mine
May make seem bare, in wanting words to show it,
But that I hope some good conceit of thine
In thy soul's thought, all naked, will bestow it;
Till whatsoever star that guides my moving
Points on me graciously with fair aspect,
And puts apparel on my tattered loving
To show me worthy of thy sweet respect.
Then may I dare to boast how I do love thee;
Till then not show my head where thou mayst prove me.

❧ 27 ❧

Weary with toil, I haste me to my bed,
The dear repose for limbs with travel tired;
But then begins a journey in my head
To work my mind when body's work's expired;
For then my thoughts, from far where I abide,
Intend a zealous pilgrimage to thee,
And keep my drooping eyelids open wide,
Looking on darkness which the blind do see;
Save that my soul's imaginary sight
Presents thy shadow to my sightless view,
Which, like a jewel hung in ghastly night,
Makes black night beauteous and her old face new.
Lo, thus, by day my limbs, by night my mind,
For thee, and for myself, no quiet find.

🎕 28 🎕

How can I then return in happy plight
That am debarr'd the benefit of rest?
When day's oppression is not eas'd by night,
But day by night and night by day oppress'd?
And each, though enemies to either's reign,
Do in consent shake hands to torture me,
The one by toil, the other to complain
How far I toil, still farther off from thee.
I tell the day, to please him, thou art bright
And dost him grace when clouds do blot the heaven;
So flatter I the swart-complexion'd night,
When sparkling stars twire not, thou gild'st the even.
But day doth daily draw my sorrows longer,
And night doth nightly make grief's strength seem stronger.

❧ 29 ❧

When in disgrace with Fortune and men's eyes,
I all alone beweep my outcast state,
And trouble deaf heaven with my bootless cries,
And look upon myself, and curse my fate,
Wishing me like to one more rich in hope,
Featur'd like him, like him with friends possess'd,
Desiring this man's art, and that man's scope,
With what I most enjoy contented least;
Yet in these thoughts myself almost despising,
Haply I think on thee, and then my state,
Like to the lark at break of day arising
From sullen earth, sings hymns at heaven's gate;
For thy sweet love rememb'red such wealth brings
That then I scorn to change my state with kings.

❦ 30 ❦

When to the sessions of sweet silent thought
I summon up remembrance of things past,
I sigh the lack of many a thing I sought,
And with old woes new wail my dear time's waste.
Then can I drown an eye, unus'd to flow,
For precious friends hid in death's dateless night,
And weep afresh love's long since cancell'd woe,
And moan th' expense of many a vanish'd sight.
Then can I grieve at grievances foregone,
And heavily from woe to woe tell o'er
The sad account of fore-bemoaned moan,
Which I new pay as if not paid before.
But if the while I think on thee, dear friend,
All losses are restor'd, and sorrows end.

❧ 31 ❧

Thy bosom is endeared with all hearts
Which I by lacking have supposed dead;
And there reigns love and all love's loving parts,
And all those friends which I thought buried.
How many a holy and obsequious tear
Hath dear religious love stol'n from mine eye,
As interest of the dead, which now appear
But things remov'd that hidden in thee lie!
Thou art the grave where buried love doth live,
Hung with the trophies of my lovers gone,
Who all their parts of me to thee did give;
That due of many now is thine alone.
Their images I lov'd I view in thee,
And thou, all they, hast all the all of me.

❧ 32 ❧

If thou survive my well-contented day
When that churl Death my bones with dust shall cover,
And shalt by fortune once more re-survey
These poor rude lines of thy deceased lover,
Compare them with the bett'ring of the time,
And though they be outstripp'd by every pen,
Reserve them for my love, not for their rhyme,
Exceeded by the height of happier men.
O, then vouchsafe me but this loving thought:
'Had my friend's Muse grown with this growing age,
A dearer birth than this his love had brought,
To march in ranks of better equipage;
But since he died, and poets better prove,
Theirs for their style I'll read, his for his love'.

❧ 33 ❧

Full many a glorious morning have I seen
Flatter the mountain-tops with sovereign eye,
Kissing with golden face the meadows green,
Gilding pale streams with heavenly alchemy;
Anon permit the basest clouds to ride
With ugly rack on his celestial face,
And from the forlorn world his visage hide,
Stealing unseen to west with this disgrace.
Even so my sun one early morn did shine
With all triumphant splendour on my brow;
But out, alack! he was but one hour mine,
The region cloud hath mask'd him from me now.
Yet him for this my love no whit disdaineth;
Suns of the world may stain when heaven's sun staineth.

✦ 34 ✦

Why didst thou promise such a beauteous day,
And make me travel forth without my cloak,
To let base clouds o'ertake me in my way,
Hiding thy brav'ry in their rotten smoke?
'Tis not enough that through the cloud thou break
To dry the rain on my storm-beaten face,
For no man well of such a salve can speak
That heals the wound, and cures not the disgrace.
Nor can thy shame give physic to my grief;
Though thou repent, yet I have still the loss.
Th' offender's sorrow lends but weak relief
To him that bears the strong offence's cross.
Ah! but those tears are pearl which thy love sheds,
And they are rich, and ransom all ill deeds.

❧ 35 ❧

No more be griev'd at that which thou hast done:
Roses have thorns, and silver fountains mud;
Clouds and eclipses stain both moon and sun,
And loathsome canker lives in sweetest bud.
All men make faults, and even I in this,
Authorizing thy trespass with compare,
Myself corrupting, salving thy amiss,
Excusing thy sins more than thy sins are;
For to thy sensual fault I bring in sense—
Thy adverse party is thy advocate—
And 'gainst myself a lawful plea commence;
Such civil war is in my love and hate
That I an accessary needs must be
To that sweet thief which sourly robs from me.

❧ 36 ❧

Let me confess that we two must be twain,
Although our undivided loves are one;
So shall those blots that do with me remain,
Without thy help, by me be borne alone.
In our two loves there is but one respect,
Though in our lives a separable spite,
Which though it alter not love's sole effect,
Yet doth it steal sweet hours from love's delight.
I may not evermore acknowledge thee,
Lest my bewailed guilt should do thee shame;
Nor thou with public kindness honour me,
Unless thou take that honour from thy name.
But do not so; I love thee in such sort
As, thou being mine, mine is thy good report.

✣ 37 ✣

As a decrepit father takes delight
To see his active child do deeds of youth,
So I, made lame by Fortune's dearest spite,
Take all my comfort of thy worth and truth;
For whether beauty, birth, or wealth, or wit,
Or any of these all, or all, or more,
Entitled in thy parts do crowned sit,
I make my love engrafted to this store.
So then I am not lame, poor, nor despis'd,
Whilst that this shadow doth such substance give
That I in thy abundance am suffic'd,
And by a part of all thy glory live.
Look what is best, that best I wish in thee;
This wish I have; then ten times happy me!

❧ 38 ❧

How can my Muse want subject to invent,
While thou dost breathe that pour'st into my verse
Thine own sweet argument, too excellent
For every vulgar paper to rehearse?
O, give thyself the thanks if aught in me
Worthy perusal stand against thy sight;
For who's so dumb that cannot write to thee,
When thou thy self dost give invention light?
Be thou the tenth Muse, ten times more in worth
Than those old nine which rhymers invocate;
And he that calls on thee, let him bring forth
Eternal numbers to outlive long date.
If my slight Muse do please these curious days,
The pain be mine, but thine shall be the praise.

39

O, how thy worth with manners may I sing,
When thou art all the better part of me?
What can mine own praise to mine own self bring?
And what is't but mine own, when I praise thee?
Even for this let us divided live,
And our dear love lose name of single one,
That by this separation I may give
That due to thee which thou deserv'st alone.
O absence, what a torment wouldst thou prove,
Were it not thy sour leisure gave sweet leave
To entertain the time with thoughts of love;
Which time and thoughts so sweetly doth deceive,
And that thou teachest how to make one twain,
By praising him here who doth hence remain!

✤ 40 ✤

Take all my loves, my love, yea, take them all;
What hast thou then more than thou hadst before?
No love, my love, that thou mayst true love call;
All mine was thine before thou hadst this more.
Then if for my love thou my love receivest,
I cannot blame thee, for my love thou usest;
But yet be blam'd, if thou thyself deceivest
By wilful taste of what thyself refusest.
I do forgive thy robb'ry, gentle thief,
Although thou steal thee all my poverty;
And yet love knows it is a greater grief
To bear love's wrong than hate's known injury.
Lascivious grace, in whom all ill well shows,
Kill me with spites; yet we must not be foes.

❧ 41 ❧

Those pretty wrongs that liberty commits
When I am sometime absent from thy heart,
Thy beauty and thy years full well befits,
For still temptation follows where thou art.
Gentle thou art, and therefore to be won,
Beauteous thou art, therefore to be assailed;
And when a woman woos, what woman's son
Will sourly leave her till she have prevailed?
Ay me! but yet thou mightst my seat forbear,
And chide thy beauty and thy straying youth,
Who lead thee in their riot even there
Where thou art forc'd to break a twofold truth:
Hers, by thy beauty tempting her to thee,
Thine, by thy beauty being false to me.

see later

❦ 42 ❦

That thou hast her, it is not all my grief,
And yet it may be said I lov'd her dearly;
That she hath thee is of my wailing chief,
A loss in love that touches me more nearly.
Loving offenders, thus I will excuse ye:
Thou dost love her because thou know'st I love her,
And for my sake even so doth she abuse me,
Suff'ring my friend for my sake to approve her.
If I lose thee, my loss is my love's gain,
And, losing her, my friend hath found that loss;
Both find each other, and I lose both twain,
And both for my sake lay on me this cross.
But here's the joy: my friend and I are one;
Sweet flattery! then she loves but me alone.

❧ 43 ❧

When most I wink, then do mine eyes best see,
For all the day they view things unrespected;
But when I sleep, in dreams they look on thee,
And, darkly bright, are bright in dark directed;
Then thou whose shadow shadows doth make bright,
How would thy shadow's form form happy show
To the clear day with thy much clearer light,
When to unseeing eyes thy shade shines so!
How would, I say, mine eyes be blessed made
By looking on thee in the living day,
When in dead night thy fair imperfect shade
Through heavy sleep on sightless eyes doth stay!
All days are nights to see till I see thee,
And nights bright days when dreams do show thee me.

❦ 44 ❧

If the dull substance of my flesh were thought,
Injurious distance should not stop my way;
For then, despite of space, I would be brought
From limits far remote, where thou dost stay.
No matter then, although my foot did stand
Upon the farthest earth remov'd from thee,
For nimble thought can jump both sea and land
As soon as think the place where he would be.
But ah! thought kills me that I am not thought,
To leap large lengths of miles when thou art gone,
But that, so much of earth and water wrought,
I must attend time's leisure with my moan,
Receiving nought by elements so slow
But heavy tears, badges of either's woe.

🏶 45 🏶

The other two, slight air and purging fire,
Are both with thee, wherever I abide;
The first my thought, the other my desire,
These present-absent with swift motion slide.
For when these quicker elements are gone
In tender embassy of love to thee,
My life, being made of four, with two alone
Sinks down to death, oppress'd with melancholy;
Until life's composition be recured
By those swift messengers return'd from thee,
Who even but now come back again, assured
Of thy fair health, recounting it to me.
This told, I joy; but then no longer glad,
I send them back again, and straight grow sad.

✦ 46 ✦

Mine eye and heart are at a mortal war
How to divide the conquest of thy sight;
Mine eye my heart thy picture's sight would bar,
My heart mine eye the freedom of that right.
My heart doth plead that thou in him dost lie,
A closet never pierc'd with crystal eyes;
But the defendant doth that plea deny,
And says in him thy fair appearance lies.
To 'cide this title is impanelled
A quest of thoughts, all tenants to the heart;
And by their verdict is determined
The clear eye's moiety and the dear heart's part—
As thus: mine eye's due is thine outward part,
And my heart's right thine inward love of heart.

❧ 47 ❧

Betwixt mine eye and heart a league is took,
And each doth good turns now unto the other.
When that mine eye is famish'd for a look,
Or heart in love with sighs himself doth smother;
With my love's picture then my eye doth feast,
And to the painted banquet bids my heart;
Another time mine eye is my heart's guest,
And in his thoughts of love doth share a part;
So, either by thy picture or my love,
Thyself away art present still with me;
For thou not farther than my thoughts canst move,
And I am still with them, and they with thee;
Or if they sleep, thy picture in my sight
Awakes my heart to heart's and eye's delight.

❧ 48 ❧

How careful was I when I took my way,
Each trifle under truest bars to thrust,
That to my use it might unused stay
From hands of falsehood, in sure wards of trust!
But thou, to whom my jewels trifles are,
Most worthy comfort, now my greatest grief,
Thou, best of dearest, and mine only care,
Art left the prey of every vulgar thief.
Thee have I not lock'd up in any chest,
Save where thou art not, though I feel thou art,
Within the gentle closure of my breast,
From whence at pleasure thou mayst come and part;
And even thence thou wilt be stol'n, I fear,
For truth proves thievish for a prize so dear.

❧ 49 ❧

Against that time, if ever that time come,
When I shall see thee frown on my defects,
When as thy love hath cast his utmost sum,
Call'd to that audit by advis'd respects;
Against that time when thou shalt strangely pass
And scarcely greet me with that sun, thine eye,
When love, converted from the thing it was,
Shall reasons find of settled gravity—
Against that time do I ensconce me here
Within the knowledge of mine own desert,
And this my hand against myself uprear,
To guard the lawful reasons on thy part:
To leave poor me thou hast the strength of laws,
Since why to love I can allege no cause.

🏵 50 🏵

How heavy do I journey on the way,
When what I seek—my weary travel's end—
Doth teach that ease and that repose to say
'Thus far the miles are measur'd from thy friend!'
The beast that bears me, tired with my woe,
Plods dully on, to bear that weight in me,
As if by some instinct the wretch did know
His rider lov'd not speed being made from thee.
The bloody spur cannot provoke him on
That sometimes anger thrusts into his hide,
Which heavily he answers with a groan,
More sharp to me than spurring to his side;
For that same groan doth put this in my mind:
My grief lies onward, and my joy behind.

✤ 51 ✤

Thus can my love excuse the slow offence
Of my dull bearer, when from thee I speed:
From where thou art why should I haste me thence?
Till I return, of posting is no need.
O, what excuse will my poor beast then find,
When swift extremity can seem but slow?
Then should I spur, though mounted on the wind;
In winged speed no motion shall I know.
Then can no horse with my desire keep pace;
Therefore desire, of perfect'st love being made,
Shall weigh no dull flesh in his fiery race;
But love, for love, thus shall excuse my jade;
Since from thee going he went wilful slow,
Towards thee I'll run, and give him leave to go.

❦ 52 ❦

So am I as the rich whose blessed key
Can bring him to his sweet up-locked treasure,
The which he will not ev'ry hour survey,
For blunting the fine point of seldom pleasure.
Therefore are feasts so solemn and so rare,
Since seldom coming, in the long year set,
Like stones of worth they thinly placed are,
Or captain jewels in the carcanet.
So is the time that keeps you as my chest,
Or as the wardrobe which the robe doth hide,
To make some special instant special blest
By new unfolding his imprison'd pride.
Blessed are you, whose worthiness gives scope,
Being had, to triumph, being lack'd, to hope.

❦ 53 ❦

What is your substance, whereof are you made,
That millions of strange shadows on you tend?
Since every one hath, every one, one shade,
And you, but one, can every shadow lend.
Describe Adonis, and the counterfeit
Is poorly imitated after you;
On Helen's cheek all art of beauty set,
And you in Grecian tires are painted new.
Speak of the spring and foison of the year:
The one doth shadow of your beauty show,
The other as your bounty doth appear,
And you in every blessed shape we know.
In all external grace you have some part,
But you like none, none you, for constant heart.

❦ 54 ❦

O, how much more doth beauty beauteous seem
By that sweet ornament which truth doth give!
The rose looks fair, but fairer we it deem
For that sweet odour which doth in it live.
The canker-blooms have full as deep a dye
As the perfumed tincture of the roses,
Hang on such thorns, and play as wantonly
When summer's breath their masked buds discloses;
But for their virtue only is their show,
They lived unwoo'd, and unrespected fade;
Die to themselves. Sweet roses do not so:
Of their sweet deaths are sweetest odours made.
And so of you, beauteous and lovely youth,
When that shall vade, by verse distills your truth.

🦢 55 🦢

Not marble nor the gilded monuments
Of princes shall outlive this pow'rful rhyme;
But you shall shine more bright in these contents
Than unswept stone, besmear'd with sluttish time.
When wasteful war shall statues overturn,
And broils root out the work of masonry,
Nor Mars his sword nor war's quick fire shall burn
The living record of your memory.
'Gainst death and all-oblivious enmity
Shall you pace forth; your praise shall still find room,
Even in the eyes of all posterity
That wear this world out to the ending doom.
So, till the judgment that yourself arise,
You live in this, and dwell in lovers' eyes.

✧ 56 ✧

Sweet love, renew thy force; be it not said
Thy edge should blunter be than appetite,
Which but to-day by feeding is allay'd,
To-morrow sharp'ned in his former might.
So, love, be thou; although to-day thou fill
Thy hungry eyes, even till they wink with fulness,
To-morrow see again, and do not kill
The spirit of love with a perpetual dulness.
Let this sad int'rim like the ocean be
Which parts the shore where two contracted new
Come daily to the banks, that, when they see
Return of love, more blest may be the view;
Or call it winter, which, being full of care,
Makes summer's welcome thrice more wish'd, more rare.

❧ 57 ❧

Being your slave, what should I do but tend
Upon the hours and times of your desire?
I have no precious time at all to spend,
Nor services to do, till you require.
Nor dare I chide the world-without-end hour,
Whilst I, my sovereign, watch the clock for you,
Nor think the bitterness of absence sour,
When you have bid your servant once adieu;
Nor dare I question with my jealous thought
Where you may be, or your affairs suppose,
But, like a sad slave, stay and think of nought
Save where you are how happy you make those.
So true a fool is love that in your will,
Though you do anything, he thinks no ill.

❧ 58 ❧

That god forbid that made me first your slave
I should in thought control your times of pleasure,
Or at your hand th' account of hours to crave,
Being your vassal bound to stay your leisure!
O, let me suffer, being at your beck,
Th' imprison'd absence of your liberty,
And patience, tame to sufferance, bide each check
Without accusing you of injury.
Be where you list; your charter is so strong
That you yourself may privilege your time
To what you will; to you it doth belong
Your self to pardon of self-doing crime.
I am to wait, though waiting so be hell;
Not blame your pleasure, be it ill or well.

❧ 59 ❧

If there be nothing new, but that which is
Hath been before, how are our brains beguil'd,
Which labouring for invention bear amiss
The second burthen of a former child!
O, that record could with a backward look,
Even of five hundred courses of the sun,
Show me your image in some antique book,
Since mind at first in character was done!
That I might see what the old world could say
To this composed wonder of your frame;
Whether we are mended, or whe'er better they,
Or whether revolution be the same.
O, sure I am, the wits of former days
To subjects worse have given admiring praise.

❦ 60 ❦

Like as the waves make towards the pebbled shore,
So do our minutes hasten to their end;
Each changing place with that which goes before,
In sequent toil all forwards do contend.
Nativity, once in the main of light,
Crawls to maturity, wherewith being crown'd,
Crooked eclipses 'gainst his glory fight,
And Time that gave doth now his gift confound.
Time doth transfix the flourish set on youth,
And delves the parallels in beauty's brow,
Feeds on the rarities of nature's truth,
And nothing stands but for his scythe to mow.
And yet to times in hope my verse shall stand,
Praising thy worth, despite his cruel hand.

❧ 61 ❧

Is it thy will thy image should keep open
My heavy eyelids to the weary night?
Dost thou desire my slumbers should be broken,
While shadows like to thee do mock my sight?
Is it thy spirit that thou send'st from thee
So far from home into my deeds to pry,
To find out shames and idle hours in me,
The scope and tenour of thy jealousy?
O no! thy love, though much, is not so great:
It is my love that keeps mine eye awake;
Mine own true love that doth my rest defeat
To play the watchman ever for thy sake.
For thee watch I, whilst thou dost wake elsewhere,
From me far off, with others all too near.

❧ 62 ❧

Sin of self-love possesseth all mine eye,
And all my soul, and all my every part;
And for this sin there is no remedy,
It is so grounded inward in my heart.
Methinks no face so gracious is as mine,
No shape so true, no truth of such account,
And for myself mine own worth do define
As I all other in all worths surmount.
But when my glass shows me myself indeed,
Beated and chopt with tann'd antiquity,
Mine own self-love quite contrary I read;
Self so self-loving were iniquity.
'Tis thee, my self, that for myself I praise,
Painting my age with beauty of thy days.

63

Against my love shall be as I am now,
With Time's injurious hand crush'd and o'erworn;
When hours have drain'd his blood, and fill'd his brow
With lines and wrinkles; when his youthful morn
Hath travell'd on to age's steepy night;
And all those beauties whereof now he's king
Are vanishing or vanish'd out of sight,
Stealing away the treasure of his spring—
For such a time do I now fortify
Against confounding age's cruel knife,
That he shall never cut from memory
My sweet love's beauty, though my lover's life.
His beauty shall in these black lines be seen,
And they shall live, and he in them still green.

❧ 64 ❧

When I have seen by Time's fell hand defaced
The rich proud cost of outworn buried age;
When sometime lofty towers I see downrased,
And brass eternal slave to mortal rage;
When I have seen the hungry ocean gain
Advantage on the kingdom of the shore,
And the firm soil win of the wat'ry main,
Increasing store with loss, and loss with store;
When I have seen such interchange of state,
Or state itself confounded to decay;
Ruin hath taught me thus to ruminate—
That Time will come and take my love away.
This thought is as a death, which cannot choose
But weep to have that which it fears to lose.

❧ 65 ❧

Since brass, nor stone, nor earth, nor boundless sea,
But sad mortality o'ersways their power,
How with this rage shall beauty hold a plea,
Whose action is no stronger than a flower?
O, how shall summer's honey breath hold out
Against the wrackful siege of batt'ring days,
When rocks impregnable are not so stout,
Nor gates of steel so strong, but Time decays?
O fearful meditation! Where, alack,
Shall Time's best jewel from Time's chest lie hid?
Or what strong hand can hold his swift foot back?
Or who his spoil of beauty can forbid?
O, none, unless this miracle have might,
That in black ink my love may still shine bright.

❧ 66 ❧

Tir'd with all these, for restful death I cry:
As, to behold desert a beggar born,
And needy nothing trimm'd in jollity,
And purest faith unhappily forsworn,
And gilded honour shamefully misplac'd,
And maiden virtue rudely strumpeted,
And right perfection wrongfully disgrac'd,
And strength by limping sway disabled,
And art made tongue-tied by authority,
And folly, doctor-like, controlling skill,
And simple truth miscall'd simplicity,
And captive good attending captain ill—
Tir'd with all these, from these would I be gone,
Save that, to die, I leave my love alone.

❦ 67 ❦

Ah! wherefore with infection should he live
And with his presence grace impiety,
That sin by him advantage should achieve,
And lace itself with his society?
Why should false painting imitate his cheek,
And steal dead seeming of his living hue?
Why should poor beauty indirectly seek
Roses of shadow, since his rose is true?
Why should he live now Nature bankrupt is,
Beggar'd of blood to blush through lively veins?
For she hath no exchequer now but his,
And, proud of many, lives upon his gains.
O, him she stores, to show what wealth she had
In days long since, before these last so bad.

🎇 68 🎇

Thus is his cheek the map of days outworn,
When beauty liv'd and died as flowers do now,
Before these bastard signs of fair were born,
Or durst inhabit on a living brow;
Before the golden tresses of the dead,
The right of sepulchres, were shorn away
To live a second life on second head,
Ere beauty's dead fleece made another gay.
In him those holy antique hours are seen,
Without all ornament, itself and true,
Making no summer of another's green,
Robbing no old to dress his beauty new;
And him as for a map doth Nature store,
To show false Art what beauty was of yore.

69

Those parts of thee that the world's eye doth view
Want nothing that the thought of hearts can mend.
All tongues, the voice of souls, give thee that due,
Utt'ring bare truth, even so as foes commend.
Thine outward thus with outward praise is crown'd;
But those same tongues that give thee so thine own
In other accents do this praise confound
By seeing farther than the eye hath shown.
They look into the beauty of thy mind,
And that, in guess, they measure by thy deeds;
Then, churls, their thoughts, although their eyes were kind,
To thy fair flower add the rank smell of weeds.
But why thy odour matcheth not thy show,
The soil is this—that thou dost common grow.

❦ 70 ❧

That thou art blam'd shall not be thy defect,
For slander's mark was ever yet the fair;
The ornament of beauty is suspect,
A crow that flies in heaven's sweetest air.
So thou be good, slander doth but approve
Thy worth the greater, being woo'd of time;
For canker vice the sweetest buds doth love,
And thou present'st a pure unstained prime.
Thou hast pass'd by the ambush of young days,
Either not assail'd, or victor being charg'd;
Yet this thy praise cannot be so thy praise
To tie up envy, evermore enlarg'd.
If some suspect of ill mask'd not thy show,
Then thou alone kingdoms of hearts shouldst owe.

🙢 71 🙠

No longer mourn for me when I am dead
Than you shall hear the surly sullen bell
Give warning to the world that I am fled
From this vile world, with vilest worms to dwell.
Nay, if you read this line, remember not
The hand that writ it; for I love you so,
That I in your sweet thoughts would be forgot,
If thinking on me then should make you woe.
O, if, I say, you look upon this verse,
When I perhaps compounded am with clay,
Do not so much as my poor name rehearse,
But let your love even with my life decay;
Lest the wise world should look into your moan,
And mock you with me after I am gone.

❧ 72 ❧

O, lest the world should task you to recite
What merit liv'd in me, that you should love
After my death, dear love, forget me quite,
For you in me can nothing worthy prove;
Unless you would devise some virtuous lie,
To do more for me than mine own desert,
And hang more praise upon deceased I
Than niggard truth would willingly impart.
O, lest your true love may seem false in this,
That you for love speak well of me untrue,
My name be buried where my body is,
And live no more to shame nor me nor you!
For I am sham'd by that which I bring forth,
And so should you, to love things nothing worth.

✿ 73 ✿

That time of year thou mayst in me behold
When yellow leaves, or none, or few, do hang
Upon those boughs which shake against the cold,
Bare ruin'd choirs where late the sweet birds sang.
In me thou seest the twilight of such day
As after sunset fadeth in the west,
Which by and by black night doth take away,
Death's second self, that seals up all in rest.
In me thou seest the glowing of such fire
That on the ashes of his youth doth lie,
As the death-bed whereon it must expire,
Consum'd with that which it was nourish'd by.
This thou perceiv'st which makes thy love more strong,
To love that well which thou must leave ere long.

❧ 74 ❧

But be contented. When that fell arrest
Without all bail shall carry me away,
My life hath in this line some interest,
Which for memorial still with thee shall stay.
When thou reviewest this, thou dost review
The very part was consecrate to thee.
The earth can have but earth, which is his due;
My spirit is thine, the better part of me.
So then thou hast but lost the dregs of life,
The prey of worms, my body being dead;
The coward conquest of a wretch's knife,
Too base of thee to be remembered.
The worth of that is that which it contains,
And that is this, and this with thee remains.

❦ 75 ❦

So are you to my thoughts as food to life,
Or as sweet-season'd showers are to the ground;
And for the peace of you I hold such strife
As 'twixt a miser and his wealth is found:
Now proud as an enjoyer, and anon
Doubting the filching age will steal his treasure;
Now counting best to be with you alone,
Then better'd that the world may see my pleasure;
Sometime all full with feasting on your sight,
And by and by clean starved for a look;
Possessing or pursuing no delight
Save what is had or must from you be took.
Thus do I pine and surfeit day by day,
Or gluttoning on all, or all away.

❧ 76 ❧

Why is my verse so barren of new pride?
So far from variation or quick change?
Why, with the time, do I not glance aside
To new-found methods and to compounds strange?
Why write I still all one, ever the same,
And keep invention in a noted weed,
That every word doth almost tell my name,
Showing their birth, and where they did proceed?
O, know, sweet love, I always write of you,
And you and love are still my argument;
So all my best is dressing old words new,
Spending again what is already spent;
For as the sun is daily new and old,
So is my love still telling what is told.

🏵 77 🏵

Thy glass will show thee how thy beauties wear,
Thy dial how thy precious minutes waste;
The vacant leaves thy mind's imprint will bear,
And of this book this learning mayst thou taste.
The wrinkles which thy glass will truly show
Of mouthed graves will give thee memory;
Thou by thy dial's shady stealth mayst know
Time's thievish progress to eternity.
Look what thy memory cannot contain
Commit to these waste blanks, and thou shalt find
Those children nurs'd, deliver'd from thy brain,
To take a new acquaintance of thy mind.
These offices, so oft as thou wilt look,
Shall profit thee, and much enrich thy book.

✿ 78 ✿

So oft have I invok'd thee for my Muse,
And found such fair assistance in my verse,
As every alien pen hath got my use,
And under thee their poesy disperse.
Thine eyes, that taught the dumb on high to sing
And heavy ignorance aloft to fly,
Have added feathers to the learned's wing
And given grace a double majesty.
Yet be most proud of that which I compile,
Whose influence is thine, and born of thee:
In others' works thou dost but mend the style,
And arts with thy sweet graces graced be;
But thou art all my art, and dost advance
As high as learning my rude ignorance.

❦ 79 ❦

Whilst I alone did call upon thy aid,
My verse alone had all thy gentle grace;
But now my gracious numbers are decay'd,
And my sick Muse doth give another place.
I grant, sweet love, thy lovely argument
Deserves the travail of a worthier pen;
Yet what of thee thy poet doth invent
He robs thee of, and pays it thee again.
He lends thee virtue, and he stole that word
From thy behaviour; beauty doth he give,
And found it in thy cheek; he can afford
No praise to thee but what in thee doth live.
Then thank him not for that which he doth say,
Since what he owes thee thou thyself dost pay.

✿ 80 ✿

O, how I faint when I of you do write,
Knowing a better spirit doth use your name
And in the praise thereof spends all his might
To make me tongue-tied, speaking of your fame!
But since your worth, wide as the ocean is,
The humble as the proudest sail doth bear,
My saucy bark, inferior far to his,
On your broad main doth wilfully appear.
Your shallowest help will hold me up afloat,
Whilst he upon your soundless deep doth ride;
Or, being wreck'd, I am a worthless boat,
He of tall building and of goodly pride.
Then if he thrive, and I be cast away,
The worst was this: my love was my decay.

81

Or I shall live your epitaph to make,
Or you survive when I in earth am rotten;
From hence your memory death cannot take,
Although in me each part will be forgotten.
Your name from hence immortal life shall have,
Though I, once gone, to all the world must die;
The earth can yield me but a common grave,
When you entombed in men's eyes shall lie.
Your monument shall be my gentle verse,
Which eyes not yet created shall o'er-read;
And tongues to be your being shall rehearse,
When all the breathers of this world are dead.
You still shall live, such virtue hath my pen,
Where breath most breathes, even in the mouths of men.

✤ 82 ✤

I grant thou wert not married to my Muse,
And therefore mayst without attaint o'er look
The dedicated words which writers use
Of their fair subject, blessing every book.
Thou art as fair in knowledge as in hue,
Finding thy worth a limit past my praise,
And therefore art enforc'd to seek anew
Some fresher stamp of the time-bettering days.
And do so, love; yet when they have devis'd
What strained touches rhetoric can lend,
Thou truly fair wert truly sympathiz'd
In true plain words by thy true-telling friend;
And their gross painting might be better us'd
Where cheeks need blood; in thee it is abus'd.

❧ 83 ❧

I never saw that you did painting need,
And therefore to your fair no painting set;
I found, or thought I found, you did exceed
The barren tender of a poet's debt;
And therefore have I slept in your report,
That you your self, being extant, well might show
How far a modern quill doth come too short,
Speaking of worth, what worth in you doth grow.
This silence for my sin you did impute,
Which shall be most my glory, being dumb;
For I impair not beauty, being mute,
When others would give life, and bring a tomb.
There lives more life in one of your fair eyes
Than both your poets can in praise devise.

❧ 84 ❧

Who is it that says most which can say more
Than this rich praise—that you alone are you?
In whose confine immured is the store
Which should example where your equal grew?
Lean penury within that pen doth dwell
That to his subject lends not some small glory;
But he that writes of you, if he can tell
That you are you, so dignifies his story.
Let him but copy what in you is writ,
Not making worse what nature made so clear,
And such a counterpart shall fame his wit,
Making his style admired every where.
You to your beauteous blessings add a curse,
Being fond on praise, which makes your praises worse.

✿ 85 ✿

My tongue-tied Muse in manners holds her still,
While comments of your praise, richly compil'd,
Reserve their character with golden quill
And precious phrase by all the Muses fil'd.
I think good thoughts, whilst other write good words,
And, like unlettered clerk, still cry 'Amen'
To every hymn that able spirit affords
In polish'd form of well-refined pen.
Hearing you prais'd, I say ''Tis so, 'tis true',
And to the most of praise add something more;
But that is in my thought, whose love to you,
Though words come hindmost, holds his rank before.
Then others for the breath of words respect,
Me for my dumb thoughts, speaking in effect.

🎕 86 🎕

Was it the proud full sail of his great verse,
Bound for the prize of all-too-precious you,
That did my ripe thoughts in my brain inhearse,
Making their tomb the womb wherein they grew?
Was it his spirit, by spirits taught to write
Above a mortal pitch, that struck me dead?
No, neither he, nor his compeers by night
Giving him aid, my verse astonished.
He nor that affable familiar ghost
Which nightly gulls him with intelligence,
As victors, of my silence cannot boast:
I was not sick of any fear from thence.
But when your countenance fill'd up his line,
Then lack'd I matter; that enfeebled mine.

✤ 87 ✤

Farewell! thou art too dear for my possessing,
And like enough thou know'st thy estimate.
The charter of thy worth gives thee releasing;
My bonds in thee are all determinate.
For how do I hold thee but by thy granting?
And for that riches where is my deserving?
The cause of this fair gift in me is wanting,
And so my patent back again is swerving.
Thy self thou gav'st, thy own worth then not knowing,
Or me, to whom thou gav'st it, else mistaking;
So thy great gift, upon misprision growing,
Comes home again, on better judgment making.
Thus have I had thee, as a dream doth flatter:
In sleep a king, but waking no such matter.

❧ 88 ❧

When thou shalt be dispos'd to set me light,
And place my merit in the eye of scorn,
Upon thy side against myself I'll fight,
And prove thee virtuous, though thou art forsworn.
With mine own weakness being best acquainted,
Upon thy part I can set down a story
Of faults conceal'd, wherein I am attainted;
That thou, in losing me, shall win much glory.
And I by this will be a gainer too;
For bending all my loving thoughts on thee,
The injuries that to myself I do,
Doing thee vantage, double vantage me.
Such is my love, to thee I so belong,
That for thy right myself will bear all wrong.

✤ 89 ✤

Say that thou didst forsake me for some fault,
And I will comment upon that offence;
Speak of my lameness, and I straight will halt;
Against thy reasons making no defence.
Thou canst not, love, disgrace me half so ill,
To set a form upon desired change,
As I'll myself disgrace, knowing thy will.
I will acquaintance strangle and look strange,
Be absent from thy walks, and in my tongue
Thy sweet beloved name no more shall dwell,
Lest I, too much profane, should do it wrong,
And haply of our old acquaintance tell.
For thee, against myself I'll vow debate,
For I must ne'er love him whom thou dost hate.

❧ 90 ❧

Then hate me when thou wilt; if ever, now;
Now while the world is bent my deeds to cross,
Join with the spite of fortune, make me bow,
And do not drop in for an after-loss.
Ah, do not, when my heart hath scap'd this sorrow,
Come in the rearward of a conquer'd woe;
Give not a windy night a rainy morrow,
To linger out a purpos'd overthrow.
If thou wilt leave me, do not leave me last,
When other petty griefs have done their spite,
But in the onset come; so shall I taste
At first the very worst of fortune's might;
And other strains of woe, which now seem woe,
Compar'd with loss of thee will not seem so.

🞉 91 🞉

Some glory in their birth, some in their skill,
Some in their wealth, some in their body's force;
Some in their garments, though new-fangled ill;
Some in their hawks and hounds, some in their horse;
And every humour hath his adjunct pleasure,
Wherein it finds a joy above the rest;
But these particulars are not my measure:
All these I better in one general best.
Thy love is better than high birth to me,
Richer than wealth, prouder than garments' cost,
Of more delight than hawks and horses be;
And, having thee, of all men's pride I boast—
Wretched in this alone, that thou mayst take
All this away, and me most wretched make.

❦ 92 ❦

But do thy worst to steal thy self away,
For term of life thou art assured mine;
And life no longer than thy love will stay,
For it depends upon that love of thine.
Then need I not to fear the worst of wrongs,
When in the least of them my life hath end.
I see a better state to me belongs
Than that which on thy humour doth depend.
Thou canst not vex me with inconstant mind,
Since that my life on thy revolt doth lie.
O what a happy title do I find,
Happy to have thy love, happy to die!
But what's so blessed-fair that fears no blot?
Thou mayst be false, and yet I know it not.

✿ 93 ✿

So shall I live, supposing thou art true,
Like a deceived husband; so love's face
May still seem love to me, though alter'd new—
Thy looks with me, thy heart in other place.
For there can live no hatred in thine eye;
Therefore in that I cannot know thy change.
In many's looks the false heart's history
Is writ in moods and frowns and wrinkles strange;
But heaven in thy creation did decree
That in thy face sweet love should ever dwell;
Whate'er thy thoughts or thy heart's workings be,
Thy looks should nothing thence but sweetness tell.
How like Eve's apple doth thy beauty grow,
If thy sweet virtue answer not thy show!

❧ 94 ❧

They that have power to hurt and will do none,
That do not do the thing they most do show,
Who, moving others, are themselves as stone,
Unmoved, cold, and to temptation slow—
They rightly do inherit Heaven's graces,
And husband nature's riches from expense;
They are the lords and owners of their faces,
Others but stewards of their excellence.
The summer's flow'r is to the summer sweet
Though to itself it only live and die;
But if that flow'r with base infection meet,
The basest weed outbraves his dignity.
For sweetest things turn sourest by their deeds:
Lilies that fester smell far worse than weeds.

🕸 95 🕸

How sweet and lovely dost thou make the shame
Which, like a canker in the fragrant rose,
Doth spot the beauty of thy budding name!
O, in what sweets dost thou thy sins enclose!
That tongue that tells the story of thy days,
Making lascivious comments on thy sport,
Cannot dispraise but in a kind of praise:
Naming thy name blesses an ill report.
O, what a mansion have those vices got
Which for their habitation chose out thee,
Where beauty's veil doth cover every blot,
And all things turns to fair that eyes can see!
Take heed, dear heart, of this large privilege;
The hardest knife ill-us'd doth lose his edge.

🏵 96 🏵

Some say thy fault is youth, some wantonness;
Some say thy grace is youth and gentle sport;
Both grace and faults are lov'd of more and less:
Thou mak'st faults graces that to thee resort.
As on the finger of a throned queen
The basest jewel will be well esteem'd;
So are those errors that in thee are seen
To truths translated and for true things deem'd.
How many lambs might the stern wolf betray,
If like a lamb he could his looks translate!
How many gazers mightst thou lead away,
If thou wouldst use the strength of all thy state!
But do not so; I love thee in such sort,
As, thou being mine, mine is thy good report.

❦ 97 ❦

How like a winter hath my absence been
From thee, the pleasure of the fleeting year!
What freezings have I felt, what dark days seen!
What old December's bareness everywhere!
And yet this time remov'd was summer's time,
The teeming autumn, big with rich increase,
Bearing the wanton burden of the prime,
Like widowed wombs after their lord's decease;
Yet this abundant issue seem'd to me
But hope of orphans, and unfathered fruit;
For summer and his pleasures wait on thee,
And, thou away, the very birds are mute;
Or, if they sing, 'tis with so dull a cheer
That leaves look pale, dreading the winter's near.

🎇 98 🎇

From you have I been absent in the spring,
When proud-pied April, dress'd in all his trim,
Hath put a spirit of youth in every thing,
That heavy Saturn laugh'd and leap'd with him.
Yet nor the lays of birds, nor the sweet smell
Of different flowers in odour and in hue,
Could make me any summer's story tell,
Or from their proud lap pluck them where they grew;
Nor did I wonder at the lily's white,
Nor praise the deep vermilion in the rose:
They were but sweet, but figures of delight,
Drawn after you, you pattern of all those.
Yet seem'd it winter still, and, you away,
As with your shadow I with these did play.

❦ 99 ❦

The forward violet thus did I chide:
Sweet thief, whence didst thou steal thy sweet that smells,
If not from my love's breath? The purple pride
Which on thy soft cheek for complexion dwells
In my love's veins thou hast too grossly dy'd.
The lily I condemned for thy hand,
And buds of marjoram had stol'n thy hair;
The roses fearfully on thorns did stand,
One blushing shame, another white despair;
A third, nor red nor white, had stol'n of both,
And to his robb'ry had annex'd thy breath;
But, for his theft, in pride of all his growth
A vengeful canker eat him up to death.
More flowers I noted, yet I none could see
But sweet or colour it had stol'n from thee.

✿ 100 ✿

Where art thou, Muse, that thou forget'st so long
To speak of that which gives thee all thy might?
Spend'st thou thy fury on some worthless song,
Dark'ning thy power to lend base subjects light?
Return, forgetful Muse, and straight redeem
In gentle numbers time so idly spent;
Sing to the ear that doth thy lays esteem
And gives thy pen both skill and argument.
Rise, resty Muse, my love's sweet face survey,
If Time have any wrinkle graven there;
If any, be a satire to decay,
And make Time's spoils despised everywhere.
Give my love fame faster than Time wastes life;
So thou prevent'st his scythe and crooked knife.

❧ 101 ❧

O truant Muse, what shall be thy amends
For thy neglect of truth in beauty dy'd?
Both truth and beauty on my love depends;
So dost thou too, and therein dignified.
Make answer, Muse. Wilt thou not haply say
'Truth needs no colour with his colour fix'd;
Beauty no pencil, beauty's truth to lay;
But best is best, if never intermix'd'?
Because he needs no praise, wilt thou be dumb?
Excuse not silence so; for't lies in thee
To make him much outlive a gilded tomb,
And to be prais'd of ages yet to be.
Then do thy office, Muse. I teach thee how
To make him seem long hence as he shows now.

❧ 102 ❧

My love is strength'ned, though more weak in seeming;
I love not less, though less the show appear;
That love is merchandiz'd whose rich esteeming
The owner's tongue doth publish every where.
Our love was new, and then but in the spring,
When I was wont to greet it with my lays;
As Philomel in summer's front doth sing,
And stops her pipe in growth of riper days.
Not that the summer is less pleasant now
Than when her mournful hymns did hush the night,
But that wild music burthens every bough,
And sweets grown common lose their dear delight.
Therefore, like her, I sometime hold my tongue,
Because I would not dull you with my song.

103

Alack, what poverty my Muse brings forth,
That, having such a scope to show her pride,
The argument all bare is of more worth
Than when it hath my added praise beside!
O, blame me not, if I no more can write!
Look in your glass, and there appears a face
That over-goes my blunt invention quite,
Dulling my lines, and doing me disgrace.
Were it not sinful then, striving to mend,
To mar the subject that before was well?
For to no other pass my verses tend
Than of your graces and your gifts to tell;
And more, much more, than in my verse can sit
Your own glass shows you, when you look in it.

✼ 104 ✼

To me, fair friend, you never can be old,
For as you were when first your eye I ey'd,
Such seems your beauty still. Three winters cold
Have from the forests shook three summers' pride,
Three beauteous springs to yellow autumn turn'd
In process of the seasons have I seen,
Three April perfumes in three hot Junes burn'd,
Since first I saw you fresh, which yet are green.
Ah, yet doth beauty, like a dial-hand,
Steal from his figure, and no pace perceiv'd;
So your sweet hue, which methinks still doth stand,
Hath motion, and mine eye may be deceiv'd.
For fear of which, hear this, thou age unbred:
Ere you were born was beauty's summer dead.

105

Let not my love be call'd idolatry,
Nor my beloved as an idol show,
Since all alike my songs and praises be
To one, of one, still such, and ever so.
Kind is my love to-day, to-morrow kind,
Still constant in a wondrous excellence;
Therefore my verse, to constancy confin'd,
One thing expressing, leaves out difference.
'Fair, kind, and true' is all my argument,
'Fair, kind, and true' varying to other words;
And in this change is my invention spent,
Three themes in one, which wondrous scope affords.
Fair, kind, and true, have often liv'd alone,
Which three, till now, never kept seat in one.

❧ 106 ❧

When in the chronicle of wasted time
I see descriptions of the fairest wights,
And beauty making beautiful old rhyme
In praise of ladies dead and lovely knights,
Then, in the blazon of sweet beauty's best,
Of hand, of foot, of lip, of eye, of brow,
I see their antique pen would have express'd
Even such a beauty as you master now.
So all their praises are but prophecies
Of this our time, all you prefiguring;
And, for they look'd but with divining eyes,
They had not skill enough your worth to sing;
For we, which now behold these present days,
Have eyes to wonder, but lack tongues to praise.

❦ 107 ❧

Not mine own fears, nor the prophetic soul
Of the wide world dreaming on things to come,
Can yet the lease of my true love control,
Suppos'd as forfeit to a confin'd doom.
The mortal moon hath her eclipse endur'd,
And the sad augurs mock their own presage;
Incertainties now crown themselves assur'd,
And peace proclaims olives of endless age.
Now with the drops of this most balmy time
My love looks fresh, and Death to me subscribes,
Since spite of him I'll live in this poor rhyme,
While he insults o'er dull and speechless tribes.
And thou in this shalt find thy monument,
When tyrants' crests and tombs of brass are spent.

❧ 108 ❧

What's in the brain that ink may character
Which hath not figur'd to thee my true spirit?
What's new to speak, what new to register,
That may express my love or thy dear merit?
Nothing, sweet boy; but yet, like prayers divine,
I must each day say o'er the very same;
Counting no old thing old, thou mine, I thine,
Even as when first I hallowed thy fair name.
So that eternal love in love's fresh case
Weighs not the dust and injury of age,
Nor gives to necessary wrinkles place,
But makes antiquity for aye his page;
Finding the first conceit of love there bred,
Where time and outward form would show it dead.

❦ 109 ❦

O, never say that I was false of heart,
Though absence seem'd my flame to qualify!
As easy might I from my self depart
As from my soul, which in thy breast doth lie:
That is my home of love. If I have rang'd,
Like him that travels, I return again,
Just to the time, not with the time exchang'd,
So that my self bring water for my stain.
Never believe, though in my nature reign'd
All frailties that besiege all kinds of blood,
That it could so preposterously be stain'd
To leave for nothing all thy sum of good;
For nothing this wide universe I call
Save thou, my rose; in it thou art my all.

❧ 110 ❧

Alas, 'tis true I have gone here and there
And made myself a motley to the view,
Gor'd mine own thoughts, sold cheap what is most dear,
Made old offences of affections new.
Most true it is that I have look'd on truth
Askance and strangely; but, by all above,
These blenches gave my heart another youth,
And worse essays prov'd thee my best of love.
Now all is done, have what shall have no end;
Mine appetite I never more will grind
On newer proof, to try an older friend,
A god in love, to whom I am confin'd.
Then give me welcome, next my heaven the best,
Even to thy pure and most most loving breast.

🎇 111 🎇

O, for my sake do you with Fortune chide,
The guilty goddess of my harmful deeds,
That did not better for my life provide
Than public means which public manners breeds.
Thence comes it that my name receives a brand,
And almost thence my nature is subdu'd
To what it works in, like the dyer's hand.
Pity me then, and wish I were renew'd;
Whilst, like a willing patient, I will drink
Potions of eisel, 'gainst my strong infection;
No bitterness that I will bitter think,
Nor double penance, to correct correction.
Pity me then, dear friend, and I assure ye,
Even that your pity is enough to cure me.

❦ 112 ❦

Your love and pity doth th' impression fill
Which vulgar scandal stamp'd upon my brow;
For what care I who calls me well or ill,
So you o'ergreen my bad, my good allow?
You are my all the world, and I must strive
To know my shames and praises from your tongue;
None else to me, nor I to none alive,
That my steel'd sense or changes right or wrong.
In so profound abysm I throw all care
Of others' voices that my adder's sense
To critic and to flatterer stopped are.
Mark how with my neglect I do dispense:
You are so strongly in my purpose bred
That all the world besides methinks are dead.

❦ 113 ❧

Since I left you, mine eye is in my mind;
And that which governs me to go about
Doth part his function, and is partly blind,
Seems seeing, but effectually is out;
For it no form delivers to the heart
Of bird, of flow'r, or shape, which it doth latch;
Of his quick objects hath the mind no part,
Nor his own vision holds what it doth catch;
For if it see the rud'st or gentlest sight,
The most sweet favour or deformed'st creature,
The mountain or the sea, the day or night,
The crow or dove, it shapes them to your feature.
Incapable of more, replete with you,
My most true mind thus mak'th mine eye untrue.

❧ 114 ❧

Or whether doth my mind, being crown'd with you,
Drink up the monarch's plague, this flattery?
Or whether shall I say mine eye saith true,
And that your love taught it this alchemy
To make of monsters and things indigest
Such cherubins as your sweet self resemble,
Creating every bad a perfect best
As fast as objects to his beams assemble?
O, 'tis the first; 'tis flatt'ry in my seeing,
And my great mind most kingly drinks it up.
Mine eye well knows what with his gust is 'greeing,
And to his palate doth prepare the cup.
If it be poison'd, 'tis the lesser sin
That mine eye loves it, and doth first begin.

❧ 115 ❧

Those lines that I before have writ do lie;
Even those that said I could not love you dearer;
Yet then my judgment knew no reason why
My most full flame should afterwards burn clearer.
But reckoning Time, whose million'd accidents
Creep in 'twixt vows and change decrees of kings,
Tan sacred beauty, blunt the sharp'st intents,
Divert strong minds to th' course of alt'ring things—
Alas, why, fearing of Time's tyranny,
Might I not then say 'Now I love you best'
When I was certain o'er incertainty,
Crowning the present, doubting of the rest?
Love is a babe; then might I not say so,
To give full growth to that which still doth grow?

❧ 116 ❧

Let me not to the marriage of true minds
Admit impediments. Love is not love
Which alters when it alteration finds,
Or bends with the remover to remove.
O, no! it is an ever-fixed mark,
That looks on tempests and is never shaken;
It is the star to every wand'ring bark,
Whose worth's unknown, although his height be taken.
Love's not Time's fool, though rosy lips and cheeks
Within his bending sickle's compass come;
Love alters not with his brief hours and weeks,
But bears it out even to the edge of doom.
  If this be error, and upon me prov'd,
  I never writ, nor no man ever lov'd.

❧ 117 ❧

Accuse me thus: that I have scanted all
Wherein I should your great deserts repay;
Forgot upon your dearest love to call,
Whereto all bonds do tie me day by day;
That I have frequent been with unknown minds,
And given to time your own dear-purchas'd right;
That I have hoisted sail to all the winds
Which should transport me farthest from your sight.
Book both my wilfulness and errors down,
And on just proof surmise accumulate;
Bring me within the level of your frown,
But shoot not at me in your wakened hate;
Since my appeal says I did strive to prove
The constancy and virtue of your love.

❧ 118 ❧

Like as to make our appetites more keen
With eager compounds we our palate urge,
As to prevent our maladies unseen
We sicken to shun sickness when we purge;
Even so, being full of your ne'er-cloying sweetness,
To bitter sauces did I frame my feeding,
And, sick of welfare, found a kind of meetness
To be diseas'd ere that there was true needing.
Thus policy in love, t' anticipate
The ills that were not, grew to faults assured,
And brought to medicine a healthful state,
Which, rank of goodness, would by ill be cured.
But thence I learn, and find the lesson true,
Drugs poison him that so fell sick of you.

❧ 119 ❧

What potions have I drunk of Siren tears,
Distill'd from limbecks foul as hell within,
Applying fears to hopes, and hopes to fears,
Still losing when I saw my self to win!
What wretched errors hath my heart committed,
Whilst it hath thought it self so blessed never!
How have mine eyes out of their spheres been fitted
In the distraction of this madding fever!
O benefit of ill! Now I find true
That better is by evil still made better;
And ruin'd love, when it is built anew,
Grows fairer than at first, more strong, far greater.
So I return rebuk'd to my content,
And gain by ill thrice more than I have spent.

❧ 120 ❧

That you were once unkind befriends me now,
And for that sorrow which I then did feel
Needs must I under my transgression bow,
Unless my nerves were brass or hammered steel.
For if you were by my unkindness shaken,
As I by yours, y'have pass'd a hell of time;
And I, a tyrant, have no leisure taken
To weigh how once I suffered in your crime.
O that our night of woe might have rememb'red
My deepest sense how hard true sorrow hits,
And soon to you, as you to me, then tend'red
The humble salve which wounded bosoms fits!
But that your trespass now becomes a fee;
Mine ransoms yours, and yours must ransom me.

⚜ 121 ⚜

'Tis better to be vile than vile esteemed,
When not to be receives reproach of being,
And the just pleasure lost, which is so deemed
Not by our feeling, but by others' seeing.
For why should others' false adulterate eyes
Give salutation to my sportive blood?
Or on my frailties why are frailer spies,
Which in their wills count bad what I think good?
No; I am that I am; and they that level
At my abuses reckon up their own.
I may be straight though they themselves be bevel;
By their rank thoughts my deeds must not be shown,
Unless this general evil they maintain:
All men are bad, and in their badness reign.

❧ 122 ❧

Thy gift, thy tables, are within my brain
Full character'd with lasting memory,
Which shall above that idle rank remain
Beyond all date, even to eternity;
Or at the least so long as brain and heart
Have faculty by nature to subsist;
Till each to raz'd oblivion yield his part
Of thee, thy record never can be miss'd.
That poor retention could not so much hold,
Nor need I tallies thy dear love to score;
Therefore to give them from me was I bold,
To trust those tables that receive thee more.
To keep an adjunct to remember thee
Were to import forgetfulness in me.

❦ 123 ❧

No, Time, thou shalt not boast that I do change.
Thy pyramids built up with newer might
To me are nothing novel, nothing strange;
They are but dressings of a former sight.
Our dates are brief, and therefore we admire
What thou dost foist upon us that is old,
And rather make them born to our desire
Than think that we before have heard them told.
Thy registers and thee I both defy,
Not wond'ring at the present nor the past,
For thy records and what we see doth lie,
Made more or less by thy continual haste.
This I do vow, and this shall ever be:
I will be true, despite thy scythe and thee.

❦ 124 ❦

If my dear love were but the child of state,
It might for Fortune's bastard be unfather'd,
As subject to Time's love or to Time's hate,
Weeds among weeds, or flowers with flowers gather'd.
No, it was builded far from accident;
It suffers not in smiling pomp, nor falls
Under the blow of thralled discontent,
Whereto th' inviting time our fashion calls.
It fears not Policy, that heretic,
Which works on leases of short-numb'red hours,
But all alone stands hugely politic,
That it nor grows with heat nor drowns with show'rs.
To this I witness call the fools of time,
Which die for goodness, who have liv'd for crime.

❧ 125 ❧

Were't aught to me I bore the canopy,
With my extern the outward honouring,
Or laid great bases for eternity,
Which proves more short than waste or ruining?
Have I not seen dwellers on form and favour
Lose all, and more, by paying too much rent,
For compound sweet forgoing simple savour—
Pitiful thrivers, in their gazing spent?
No, let me be obsequious in thy heart,
And take thou my oblation, poor but free,
Which is not mix'd with seconds, knows no art
But mutual render, only me for thee.
Hence, thou suborn'd informer! A true soul,
When most impeach'd, stands least in thy control.

❧ 126 ❧

O thou, my lovely boy, who in thy power
Dost hold Time's fickle glass, his sickle hour;
Who hast by waning grown, and therein show'st
Thy lovers withering as thy sweet self grow'st;
If Nature, sovereign mistress over wrack,
As thou goest onwards, still will pluck thee back,
She keeps thee to this purpose, that her skill
May time disgrace, and wretched minutes kill.
Yet fear her, O thou minion of her pleasure!
She may detain, but not still keep, her treasure;
Her audit, though delay'd, answer'd must be,
And her quietus is to render thee.

❧ 127 ❧

In the old age black was not counted fair,
Or if it were, it bore not beauty's name;
But now is black beauty's successive heir,
And beauty slander'd with a bastard shame;
For since each hand hath put on nature's power,
Fairing the foul with art's false borrow'd face,
Sweet beauty hath no name, no holy bower,
But is profan'd, if not lives in disgrace.
Therefore my mistress' brows are raven black,
Her eyes so suited, and they mourners seem
At such who, not born fair, no beauty lack,
Sland'ring creation with a false esteem.
Yet so they mourn, becoming of their woe,
That every tongue says beauty should look so.

❧ 128 ❧

How oft, when thou, my music, music play'st
Upon that blessed wood whose motion sounds
With thy sweet fingers, when thou gently sway'st
The wiry concord that mine ear confounds,
Do I envy those jacks that nimble leap
To kiss the tender inward of thy hand,
Whilst my poor lips, which should that harvest reap,
At the wood's boldness by thee blushing stand!
To be so tickled, they would change their state
And situation with those dancing chips
O'er whom thy fingers walk with gentle gait,
Making dead wood more blest than living lips.
Since saucy jacks so happy are in this,
Give them thy fingers, me thy lips to kiss.

❀ 129 ❀

Th' expense of spirit in a waste of shame
Is lust in action; and till action, lust
Is perjur'd, murd'rous, bloody, full of blame,
Savage, extreme, rude, cruel, not to trust;
Enjoy'd no sooner but despised straight;
Past reason hunted, and, no sooner had,
Past reason hated, as a swallowed bait,
On purpose laid to make the taker mad—
Mad in pursuit, and in possession so;
Had, having, and in quest to have, extreme;
A bliss in proof, and prov'd, a very woe;
Before, a joy propos'd; behind, a dream.
All this the world well knows; yet none knows well
To shun the heaven that leads men to this hell.

❧ 130 ❧

My mistress' eyes are nothing like the sun;
Coral is far more red than her lips' red;
If snow be white, why then her breasts are dun;
If hairs be wires, black wires grow on her head.
I have seen roses damask'd, red and white,
But no such roses see I in her cheeks;
And in some perfumes is there more delight
Than in the breath that from my mistress reeks.
I love to hear her speak, yet well I know
That music hath a far more pleasing sound;
I grant I never saw a goddess go—
My mistress when she walks treads on the ground.
And yet, by heaven, I think my love as rare
As any she belied with false compare.

✣ 131 ✣

Thou art as tyrannous, so as thou art,
As those whose beauties proudly make them cruel;
For well thou know'st to my dear doting heart
Thou art the fairest and most precious jewel.
Yet, in good faith, some say that thee behold
Thy face hath not the power to make love groan.
To say they err I dare not be so bold,
Although I swear it to myself alone.
And, to be sure that is not false I swear,
A thousand groans, but thinking on thy face,
One on another's neck, do witness bear
Thy black is fairest in my judgment's place.
In nothing art thou black save in thy deeds,
And thence this slander, as I think, proceeds.

✤ 132 ✤

Thine eyes I love, and they, as pitying me,
Knowing thy heart torments me with disdain,
Have put on black, and loving mourners be,
Looking with pretty ruth upon my pain.
And truly not the morning sun of heaven
Better becomes the grey cheeks of the east,
Nor that full star that ushers in the even
Doth half that glory to the sober west,
As those two mourning eyes become thy face.
O, let it then as well beseem thy heart
To mourn for me, since mourning doth thee grace,
And suit thy pity like in every part.
Then will I swear beauty herself is black,
And all they foul that thy complexion lack.

❧ 133 ❧

Beshrew that heart that makes my heart to groan
For that deep wound it gives my friend and me!
Is't not enough to torture me alone,
But slave to slavery my sweet'st friend must be?
Me from my self thy cruel eye hath taken,
And my next self thou harder hast engrossed;
Of him, my self, and thee, I am forsaken;
A torment thrice three-fold thus to be crossed.
Prison my heart in thy steel bosom's ward,
But then my friend's heart let my poor heart bail;
Whoe'er keeps me, let my heart be his guard;
Thou canst not then use rigour in my gaol.
And yet thou wilt; for I, being pent in thee,
Perforce am thine, and all that is in me.

❦ 134 ❦

So now I have confess'd that he is thine,
And I myself am mortgag'd to thy will;
My self I'll forfeit, so that other mine
Thou wilt restore to be my comfort still.
But thou wilt not, nor he will not be free,
For thou art covetous, and he is kind;
He learn'd but surety-like to write for me
Under that bond that him as fast doth bind.
The statute of thy beauty thou wilt take,
Thou usurer that put'st forth all to use,
And sue a friend came debtor for my sake;
So him I lose through my unkind abuse.
Him have I lost; thou hast both him and me;
He pays the whole, and yet am I not free.

❧ 135 ❧

Whoever hath her wish, thou hast thy Will,
And Will to boot, and Will in over-plus;
More than enough am I that vex thee still,
To thy sweet will making addition thus.
Wilt thou, whose will is large and spacious,
Not once vouchsafe to hide my will in thine?
Shall will in others seem right gracious,
And in my will no fair acceptance shine?
The sea, all water, yet receives rain still,
And in abundance addeth to his store;
So thou, being rich in Will, add to thy Will
One will of mine, to make thy large Will more.
Let no unkind, no fair beseechers kill;
Think all but one, and me in that one Will.

136

If thy soul check thee that I come so near,
Swear to thy blind soul that I was thy Will,
And will, thy soul knows, is admitted there;
Thus far for love my love-suit, sweet, fulfil.
Will will fulfil the treasure of thy love,
Ay, fill it full with wills, and my will one.
In things of great receipt with ease we prove
Among a number one is reckon'd none.
Then in the number let me pass untold,
Though in thy store's account I one must be;
For nothing hold me, so it please thee hold
That nothing me, a something sweet to thee;
Make but my name thy love, and love that still,
And then thou lov'st me, for my name is Will.

❧ 137 ❧

Thou blind fool, Love, what dost thou to mine eyes
That they behold, and see not what they see?
They know what beauty is, see where it lies,
Yet what the best is take the worst to be.
If eyes, corrupt by over-partial looks,
Be anchor'd in the bay where all men ride,
Why of eyes' falsehood hast thou forged hooks,
Whereto the judgment of my heart is tied?
Why should my heart think that a several plot,
Which my heart knows the wide world's common place?
Or mine eyes, seeing this, say this is not,
To put fair truth upon so foul a face?
In things right true my heart and eyes have erred,
And to this false plague are they now transferred.

❀ 138 ❀

When my love swears that she is made of truth,
I do believe her, though I know she lies,
That she might think me some untutor'd youth,
Unlearned in the world's false subtleties.
Thus vainly thinking that she thinks me young,
Although she knows my days are past the best,
Simply I credit her false-speaking tongue;
On both sides thus is simple truth suppress'd.
But wherefore says she not she is unjust?
And wherefore say not I that I am old?
O, love's best habit is in seeming trust,
And age in love loves not to have years told.
Therefore I lie with her, and she with me,
And in our faults by lies we flattered be.

❀ 139 ❀

O, call not me to justify the wrong
That thy unkindness lays upon my heart;
Wound me not with thine eye, but with thy tongue;
Use power with power, and slay me not by art.
Tell me thou lov'st elsewhere; but in my sight,
Dear heart, forbear to glance thine eye aside.
What need'st thou wound with cunning, when thy might
Is more than my o'erpress'd defence can bide?
Let me excuse thee: ah! my love well knows
Her pretty looks have been mine enemies;
And therefore from my face she turns my foes,
That they elsewhere might dart their injuries.
Yet do not so; but since I am near slain,
Kill me outright with looks and rid my pain.

140

Be wise as thou art cruel; do not press
My tongue-tied patience with too much disdain;
Lest sorrow lend me words, and words express
The manner of my pity-wanting pain.
If I might teach thee wit, better it were,
Though not to love, yet, love, to tell me so;
As testy sick men, when their deaths be near,
No news but health from their physicians know.
For, if I should despair, I should grow mad,
And in my madness might speak ill of thee.
Now this ill-wresting world is grown so bad
Mad slanderers by mad ears believed be.
That I may not be so, nor thou belied,
Bear thine eyes straight, though thy proud heart go wide.

❧ 141 ❧

In faith, I do not love thee with mine eyes,
For they in thee a thousand errors note;
But 'tis my heart that loves what they despise,
Who in despite of view is pleas'd to dote.
Nor are mine ears with thy tongue's tune delighted;
Nor tender feeling to base touches prone,
Nor taste nor smell desire to be invited
To any sensual feast with thee alone;
But my five wits nor my five senses can
Dissuade one foolish heart from serving thee,
Who leaves unsway'd the likeness of a man,
Thy proud heart's slave and vassal wretch to be.
Only my plague thus far I count my gain,
That she that makes me sin awards me pain.

142

Love is my sin, and thy dear virtue hate,
Hate of my sin, grounded on sinful loving.
O, but with mine compare thou thine own state,
And thou shalt find it merits not reproving;
Or, if it do, not from those lips of thine,
That have profan'd their scarlet ornaments,
And seal'd false bonds of love as oft as mine;
Robb'd others' beds' revenues of their rents.
Be it lawful I love thee as thou lov'st those
Whom thine eyes woo as mine importune thee.
Root pity in thy heart, that, when it grows,
Thy pity may deserve to pitied be.
If thou dost seek to have what thou dost hide,
By self-example mayst thou be denied!

❧ 143 ❧

Lo as a careful huswife runs to catch
One of her feathered creatures broke away,
Sets down her babe, and makes all swift dispatch
In pursuit of the thing she would have stay;
Whilst her neglected child holds her in chase,
Cries to catch her whose busy care is bent
To follow that which flies before her face,
Not prizing her poor infant's discontent;
So run'st thou after that which flies from thee,
Whilst I thy babe chase thee afar behind;
But if thou catch thy hope, turn back to me,
And play the mother's part, kiss me, be kind.
So will I pray that thou mayst have thy Will,
If thou turn back and my loud crying still.

❧ 144 ❧

Two loves I have, of comfort and despair,
Which like two spirits do suggest me still;
The better angel is a man right fair,
The worser spirit a woman colour'd ill.
To win me soon to hell, my female evil
Tempteth my better angel from my side,
And would corrupt my saint to be a devil,
Wooing his purity with her foul pride.
And whether that my angel be turn'd fiend,
Suspect I may, yet not directly tell;
But being both from me, both to each friend,
I guess one angel in another's hell.
Yet this shall I ne'er know, but live in doubt,
Till my bad angel fire my good one out.

❧ 145 ❧

Those lips that Love's own hand did make
Breath'd forth the sound that said 'I hate'
To me that languish'd for her sake;
But when she saw my woeful state,
Straight in her heart did mercy come,
Chiding that tongue that ever sweet
Was us'd in giving gentle doom;
And taught it thus anew to greet:
'I hate' she alter'd with an end
That follow'd it as gentle day
Doth follow night, who like a fiend
From heaven to hell is flown away:
'I hate' from hate away she threw,
And sav'd my life, saying 'not you'.

❦ 146 ❦

Poor soul, the centre of my sinful earth,
[My sinful earth] these rebel pow'rs that thee array,
Why dost thou pine within and suffer dearth,
Painting thy outward walls so costly gay?
Why so large cost, having so short a lease,
Dost thou upon thy fading mansion spend?
Shall worms, inheritors of this excess,
Eat up thy charge? Is this thy body's end?
Then, soul, live thou upon thy servant's loss,
And let that pine to aggravate thy store;
Buy terms divine in selling hours of dross;
Within be fed, without be rich no more.
So shalt thou feed on Death, that feeds on men,
And, Death once dead, there's no more dying then.

❧ 147 ❧

My love is as a fever, longing still
For that which longer nurseth the disease;
Feeding on that which doth preserve the ill,
Th' uncertain sickly appetite to please.
My Reason, the physician to my Love,
Angry that his prescriptions are not kept,
Hath left me, and I desperate now approve
Desire is death, which physic did except.
Past cure I am, now reason is past care,
And frantic mad with evermore unrest;
My thoughts and my discourse as mad men's are,
At random from the truth vainly express'd;
For I have sworn thee fair, and thought thee bright,
Who art as black as hell, as dark as night.

❧ 148 ❧

O me, what eyes hath Love put in my head,
Which have no correspondence with true sight!
Or, if they have, where is my judgment fled,
That censures falsely what they see aright?
If that be fair whereon my false eyes dote,
What means the world to say it is not so?
If it be not, then love doth well denote
Love's eye is not so true as all men's—no,
How can it? O, how can Love's eye be true,
That is so vex'd with watching and with tears?
No marvel then though I mistake my view:
The sun itself sees not till heaven clears.
O cunning Love! with tears thou keep'st me blind,
Lest eyes well seeing thy foul faults should find.

❧ 149 ❧

Canst thou, O cruel! say I love thee not,
When I against myself with thee partake?
Do I not think on thee when I forgot
Am of myself, all tyrant, for thy sake?
Who hateth thee that I do call my friend?
On whom frown'st thou that I do fawn upon?
Nay, if thou lour'st on me, do I not spend
Revenge upon myself with present moan?
What merit do I in myself respect
That is so proud thy service to despise,
When all my best doth worship thy defect,
Commanded by the motion of thine eyes?
But, love, hate on, for now I know thy mind:
Those that can see thou lov'st, and I am blind.

✤ 150 ✤

O, from what pow'r hast thou this pow'rful might
With insufficiency my heart to sway?
To make me give the lie to my true sight,
And swear that brightness doth not grace the day?
Whence hast thou this becoming of things ill,
That in the very refuse of thy deeds
There is such strength and warrantise of skill
That in my mind thy worst all best exceeds?
Who taught thee how to make me love thee more,
The more I hear and see just cause of hate?
O, though I love what others do abhor,
With others thou shouldst not abhor my state;
If thy unworthiness rais'd love in me,
More worthy I to be belov'd of thee.

🏵 151 🏵

Love is too young to know what conscience is;
Yet who knows not conscience is born of love?
Then, gentle cheater, urge not my amiss,
Lest guilty of my faults thy sweet self prove.
For thou betraying me, I do betray
My nobler part to my gross body's treason;
My soul doth tell my body that he may
Triumph in love; flesh stays no farther reason,
But, rising at thy name, doth point out thee
As his triumphant prize. Proud of this pride,
He is contented thy poor drudge to be,
To stand in thy affairs, fall by thy side.
No want of conscience hold it that I call
Her 'love' for whose dear love I rise and fall.

❦ 152 ❦

In loving thee thou know'st I am forsworn,
But thou art twice forsworn, to me love swearing;
In act thy bed-vow broke, and new faith torn
In vowing new hate after new love bearing.
But why of two oaths' breach do I accuse thee,
When I break twenty? I am perjur'd most;
For all my vows are oaths but to misuse thee,
And all my honest faith in thee is lost;
For I have sworn deep oaths of thy deep kindness,
Oaths of thy love, thy truth, thy constancy;
And, to enlighten thee, gave eyes to blindness,
Or made them swear against the thing they see;
For I have sworn thee fair—more perjur'd I,
To swear against the truth so foul a lie!

❧ 153 ❧

Cupid laid by his brand, and fell asleep.
A maid of Dian's this advantage found,
And his love-kindling fire did quickly steep
In a cold valley-fountain of that ground;
Which borrow'd from this holy fire of Love
A dateless lively heat, still to endure,
And grew a seething bath, which yet men prove
Against strange maladies a sovereign cure.
But at my mistress' eye Love's brand new-fired,
The boy for trial needs would touch my breast;
I, sick withal, the help of bath desired,
And thither hied, a sad distemper'd guest,
But found no cure. The bath for my help lies
Where Cupid got new fire—my mistress' eyes.

✿ 154 ✿

The little love-god, lying once asleep,
Laid by his side his heart-inflaming brand,
Whilst many nymphs that vow'd chaste life to keep
Came tripping by; but in her maiden hand
The fairest votary took up that fire
Which many legions of true hearts had warm'd;
And so the general of hot desire
Was sleeping by a virgin hand disarm'd.
This brand she quenched in a cool well by,
Which from Love's fire took heat perpetual,
Growing a bath and healthful remedy
For men diseas'd; but I, my mistress' thrall,
Came there for cure, and this by that I prove:
Love's fire heats water, water cools not love.

*Plays
and
Poems*

The plays are arranged in the order of composition given in the *Riverside* edition.
The poem *Venus and Adonis* was written c. 1592 and *The Phoenix and the Turtle* c. 1601.

The Two Gentlemen of Verona

PROTEUS AND JULIA

Julia describes her love for Proteus to her maid, Lucetta.

Luc.   I do not seek to quench your love's hot fire,
But qualify the fire's extreme rage,
Lest it should burn above the bounds of reason.
Jul.   The more thou dam'st it up, the more it burns.
The current that with gentle murmur glides,
Thou know'st, being stopp'd, impatiently doth rage;
But when his fair course is not hindered,
He makes sweet music with th' enamell'd stones,
Giving a gentle kiss to every sedge
He overtaketh in his pilgrimage;
And so by many winding nooks he strays,
With willing sport, to the wild ocean.
Then let me go, and hinder not my course.
I'll be as patient as a gentle stream,
And make a pastime of each weary step,
Till the last step have brought me to my love;
And there I'll rest as, after much turmoil,
A blessed soul doth in Elysium.

(II, vii, 21–38)

VALENTINE AND SILVIA

Val. And why not death rather than living torment?
To die is to be banish'd from myself,
And Silvia is myself; banish'd from her
Is self from self, a deadly banishment.
What light is light, if Silvia be not seen?
What joy is joy, if Silvia be not by?
Unless it be to think that she is by,
And feed upon the shadow of perfection.
Except I be by Silvia in the night,
There is no music in the nightingale;
Unless I look on Silvia in the day,
There is no day for me to look upon.
She is my essence, and I leave to be
If I be not by her fair influence
Foster'd, illumin'd, cherish'd, kept alive.
I fly not death, to fly his deadly doom:
Tarry I here, I but attend on death;
But fly I hence, I fly away from life.

(*III, i, 170–187*)

Love's Labour's Lost

THE KING OF NAVARRE

Boyet describes the lovesick King to the Princess of France.

Boyet.	If my observation, which very seldom lies,
	By the heart's still rhetoric disclosed with eyes,
	Deceive me not now, Navarre is infected.
Prin.	With what?
Boyet.	With that which we lovers entitle 'affected'.
Prin.	Your reason?
Boyet.	Why, all his behaviours did make their retire
	To the court of his eye, peeping thorough desire.
	His heart, like an agate, with your print impressed,
	Proud with his form, in his eye pride expressed;
	His tongue, all impatient to speak and not see,
	Did stumble with haste in his eyesight to be;
	All senses to that sense did make their repair,
	To feel only looking on fairest of fair.
	Methought all his senses were lock'd in his eye,
	As jewels in crystal for some prince to buy;
	Who, tend'ring their own worth from where they were glass'd,
	Did point you to buy them, along as you pass'd.
	His face's own margent did quote such amazes
	That all eyes saw his eyes enchanted with gazes.

(II, i, 227–246)

BEROWNE

Ber. And I, forsooth, in love; I, that have been love's
whip;
A very beadle to a humorous sigh;
A critic, nay, a night-watch constable;
A domineering pedant o'er the boy,
Than whom no mortal so magnificent!
This wimpled, whining, purblind, wayward boy,
This senior-junior, giant-dwarf, Dan Cupid;
Regent of love-rhymes, lord of folded arms,
Th' anointed sovereign of sighs and groans,
Liege of all loiterers and malcontents,
Dread prince of plackets, king of codpieces,
Sole imperator, and great general
Of trotting paritors. O my little heart!
And I to be a corporal of his field,
And wear his colours like a tumbler's hoop!
What! I love, I sue, I seek a wife—
A woman, that is like a German clock,
Still a-repairing, ever out of frame,
And never going aright, being a watch,
But being watch'd that it may still go right!

(III, i, 164–183)

BEROWNE

Ber. O, but for my love, day would turn to night!
Of all complexions the cull'd sovereignty
Do meet, as at a fair, in her fair cheek,
Where several worthies make one dignity,
Where nothing wants that want itself doth seek.
Lend me the flourish of all gentle tongues—
Fie, painted rhetoric! O, she needs it not!
To things of sale a seller's praise belongs:
She passes praise; then praise too short doth blot.
A wither'd hermit, five-score winters worn,
Might shake off fifty, looking in her eye.
Beauty doth varnish age, as if new-born,
And gives the crutch the cradle's infancy.
O, 'tis the sun that maketh all things shine!

(*IV, iii, 229–242*)

BEROWNE

Berowne justifies love against study.

Ber. O, we have made a vow to study, lords,
And in that vow we have forsworn our books.
For when would you, my liege, or you, or you,
In leaden contemplation have found out
Such fiery numbers as the prompting eyes
Of beauty's tutors have enrich'd you with?
Other slow arts entirely keep the brain;
And therefore, finding barren practisers,
Scarce show a harvest of their heavy toil;
But love, first learned in a lady's eyes,
Lives not alone immured in the brain,
But with the motion of all elements
Courses as swift as thought in every power,
And gives to every power a double power,
Above their functions and their offices.
It adds a precious seeing to the eye:
A lover's eyes will gaze an eagle blind.
A lover's ear will hear the lowest sound,
When the suspicious head of theft is stopp'd.
Love's feeling is more soft and sensible
Than are the tender horns of cockled snails;
Love's tongue proves dainty Bacchus gross in taste.
For valour, is not Love a Hercules,
Still climbing trees in the Hesperides?
Subtle as Sphinx; as sweet and musical

LOVE'S LABOUR'S LOST

As bright Apollo's lute, strung with his hair.
And when Love speaks, the voice of all the gods
Make heaven drowsy with the harmony.
Never durst poet touch a pen to write
Until his ink were temp'red with Love's sighs;
O, then his lines would ravish savage ears,
And plant in tyrants mild humility.
From women's eyes this doctrine I derive.
They sparkle still the right Promethean fire;
They are the books, the arts, the academes,
That show, contain, and nourish, all the world,
Else none at all in aught proves excellent.

(*IV, iii, 314–350*)

Romeo and Juliet

Rom. O, she doth teach the torches to burn bright!
It seems she hangs upon the cheek of night
As a rich jewel in an Ethiop's ear—
Beauty too rich for use, for earth too dear!
So shows a snowy dove trooping with crows
As yonder lady o'er her fellows shows.
The measure done, I'll watch her place of stand,
And, touching hers, make blessed my rude hand.
Did my heart love till now? Forswear it, sight;
For I ne'er saw true beauty till this night.

(I, v, 42–51)

ROMEO AND JULIET

Rom. If I profane with my unworthiest hand
This holy shrine, the gentle fine is this:
My lips, two blushing pilgrims, ready stand
To smooth that rough touch with a tender kiss.
Jul. Good pilgrim, you do wrong your hand too
much,
Which mannerly devotion shows in this;
For saints have hands that pilgrims' hands do
touch,
And palm to palm is holy palmers' kiss.
Rom. Have not saints lips, and holy palmers too?
Jul. Ay, pilgrim, lips that they must use in pray'r.
Rom. O, then, dear saint, let lips do what hands do!
They pray; grant thou, lest faith turn to despair.
Jul. Saints do not move, though grant for prayers' sake.
Rom. Then move not while my prayer's effect I take.
Thus from my lips by thine my sin is purg'd.
(*Kissing her*)
Jul. Then have my lips the sin that they have took.
Rom. Sin from my lips? O trespass sweetly urg'd!
Give me my sin again. (*Kissing her*)
Jul. You kiss by th' book.

(*I, v, 91–108*)

Rom. But, soft! What light through yonder window breaks?
It is the east, and Juliet is the sun.
Arise, fair sun, and kill the envious moon,
Who is already sick and pale with grief
That thou her maid art far more fair than she.
Be not her maid, since she is envious;
Her vestal livery is but sick and green,
And none but fools do wear it; cast it off.
It is my lady; O, it is my love!
O that she knew she were!
She speaks, yet she says nothing. What of that?
Her eye discourses; I will answer it.
I am too bold, 'tis not to me she speaks;
Two of the fairest stars in all the heaven,
Having some business, do entreat her eyes
To twinkle in their spheres till they return.
What if her eyes were there, they in her head?
The brightness of her cheek would shame those stars,
As daylight doth a lamp; her eyes in heaven
Would through the airy region stream so bright
That birds would sing, and think it were not night.
See how she leans her cheek upon her hand!
O that I were a glove upon that hand,
That I might touch that cheek!

Jul. Ay me!

Rom. She speaks.
O, speak again, bright angel, for thou art
As glorious to this night, being o'er my head,
As is a winged messenger of heaven

ROMEO AND JULIET

Unto the white-upturned wond'ring eyes
Of mortals that fall back to gaze on him,
When he bestrides the lazy-pacing clouds
And sails upon the bosom of the air.

(*II, ii, 2–32*)

ROMEO AND JULIET

Friar Lawrence marries Romeo and Juliet.

Fri. L.	So smile the heavens upon this holy act
	That after-hours with sorrow chide us not!
Rom.	Amen, amen! But come what sorrow can,
	It cannot countervail the exchange of joy
	That one short minute gives me in her sight.
	Do thou but close our hands with holy words,
	Then love-devouring death do what he dare;
	It is enough I may but call her mine.
Fri. L.	These violent delights have violent ends,
	And in their triumph die; like fire and powder,
	Which, as thy kiss, consume. The sweetest honey
	Is loathsome in his own deliciousness,
	And in the taste confounds the appetite.
	Therefore love moderately: long love doth so;
	Too swift arrives as tardy as too slow.

(II, vi, 1–15)

Jul.   Gallop apace, you fiery-footed steeds
Towards Phœbus' lodging; such a waggoner
As Phaethon would whip you to the west,
And bring in cloudy night immediately.
Spread thy close curtain, love-performing night,
That runaways' eyes may wink, and Romeo
Leap to these arms, untalk'd of and unseen.
Lovers can see to do their amorous rites
By their own beauties; or if love be blind,
It best agrees with night. Come, civil night,
Thou sober-suited matron, all in black,
And learn me how to lose a winning match,
Play'd for a pair of stainless maidenhoods;
Hood my unmann'd blood, bating in my cheeks,
With thy black mantle, till strange love, grown bold,
Think true love acted simple modesty.
Come, night; come, Romeo; come, thou day in night;
For thou wilt lie upon the wings of night
Whiter than new snow on a raven's back.
Come, gentle night, come, loving black-brow'd night,
Give me my Romeo; and, when he shall die,
Take him and cut him out in little stars,
And he will make the face of heaven so fine
That all the world will be in love with night,
And pay no worship to the garish sun.
O, I have bought the mansion of a love,
But not possess'd it; and though I am sold,
Not yet enjoy'd. So tedious is this day
As is the night before some festival
To an impatient child that hath new robes,
And may not wear them.

                                    (III, ii, 1–31)

ROMEO AND JULIET

| Jul. | Wilt thou be gone? It is not yet near day;
It was the nightingale, and not the lark,
That pierc'd the fearful hollow of thine ear;
Nightly she sings on yond pomegranate tree.
Believe me, love, it was the nightingale. |

Rom. It was the lark, the herald of the morn,
No nightingale. Look, love, what envious streaks
Do lace the severing clouds in yonder east;
Night's candles are burnt out, and jocund day
Stands tiptoe on the misty mountain tops.
I must be gone and live, or stay and die.

Jul. Yond light is not daylight; I know it, I:
It is some meteor that the sun exhales
To be to thee this night a torch-bearer,
And light thee on thy way to Mantua;
Therefore stay yet; thou need'st not to be gone.

Rom. Let me be ta'en, let me be put to death;
I am content, so thou wilt have it so.
I'll say yon grey is not the morning's eye,
'Tis but the pale reflex of Cynthia's brow;
Nor that is not the lark whose notes do beat
The vaulty heaven so high above our heads.
I have more care to stay than will to go.
Come death, and welcome! Juliet wills it so.
How is't, my soul? Let's talk—it is not day.

Jul. It is, it is; hie hence, be gone, away!
It is the lark that sings so out of tune,
Straining harsh discords and unpleasing sharps.
Some say the lark makes sweet division;
This doth not so, for she divideth us.
Some say the lark and loathed toad change eyes;

O, now I would they had chang'd voices too!
Since arm from arm that voice doth us affray,
Hunting thee hence with hunts-up to the day.
O, now be gone! More light and light it grows.
Rom. More light and light—more dark and dark our
woes!

(III, v, 1–36)

A Midsummer Night's Dream

HERMIA AND LYSANDER

Lys.	Ay me! for aught that I could ever read,
	Could ever hear by tale or history,
	The course of true love never did run smooth;
	But either it was different in blood—
Her.	O cross! too high to be enthrall'd to low.
Lys.	Or else misgraffed in respect of years—
Her.	O spite! too old to be engag'd to young.
Lys.	Or else it stood upon the choice of friends—
Her.	O hell! to choose love by another's eyes.
Lys.	Or, if there were a sympathy in choice,
	War, death, or sickness, did lay siege to it,
	Making it momentary as a sound,
	Swift as a shadow, short as any dream,
	Brief as the lightning in the collied night
	That, in a spleen, unfolds both heaven and earth,
	And ere a man hath power to say 'Behold!'
	The jaws of darkness do devour it up;
	So quick bright things come to confusion.
Her.	If then true lovers have been ever cross'd,
	It stands as an edict in destiny.
	Then let us teach our trial patience,
	Because it is a customary cross,
	As due to love as thoughts and dreams and sighs,
	Wishes and tears, poor Fancy's followers.

(*I, i, 132–155*)

HELENA AND DEMETRIUS

Hel.   How happy some o'er other some can be!
       Through Athens I am thought as fair as she.
       But what of that? Demetrius thinks not so;
       He will not know what all but he do know.
       And as he errs, doting on Hermia's eyes,
       So I, admiring of his qualities.
       Things base and vile, holding no quantity,
       Love can transpose to form and dignity.
       Love looks not with the eyes, but with the mind;
       And therefore is wing'd Cupid painted blind.
       Nor hath Love's mind of any judgment taste;
       Wings and no eyes figure unheedy haste;
       And therefore is Love said to be a child,
       Because in choice he is so oft beguil'd.
       As waggish boys in game themselves forswear,
       So the boy Love is perjur'd everywhere;
       For ere Demetrius look'd on Hermia's eyne,
       He hail'd down oaths that he was only mine;
       And when this hail some heat from Hermia felt,
       So he dissolv'd, and show'rs of oaths did melt.

                                         (*I, i, 226–245*)

THESEUS

The.   Lovers and madmen have such seething brains,
Such shaping fantasies, that apprehend
More than cool reason ever comprehends.
The lunatic, the lover, and the poet,
Are of imagination all compact.
One sees more devils than vast hell can hold;
That is the madman. The lover, all as frantic,
Sees Helen's beauty in a brow of Egypt.
The poet's eye, in a fine frenzy rolling,
Doth glance from heaven to earth, from earth to
heaven;
And as imagination bodies forth
The forms of things unknown, the poet's pen
Turns them to shapes, and gives to airy nothing
A local habitation and a name.

(V, i, 4–17)

The Merchant of Venice

PORTIA

Por. Tell me where is fancy bred,
Or in the heart or in the head,
How begot, how nourished?
Reply, reply.
It is engend'red in the eyes,
With gazing fed; and fancy dies
In the cradle where it lies.
Let us all ring fancy's knell:
I'll begin it—Ding, dong, bell.

(*III, ii, 63–71*)

PORTIA AND BASSANIO

Bass.   What find I here?
        Fair Portia's counterfeit! What demi–god
        Hath come so near creation? Move these eyes?
        Or whether riding on the balls of mine
        Seem they in motion? Here are sever'd lips,
        Parted with sugar breath; so sweet a bar
        Should sunder such sweet friends. Here in her hairs
        The painter plays the spider, and hath woven
        A golden mesh t' entrap the hearts of men
        Faster than gnats in cobwebs. But her eyes—
        How could he see to do them? Having made one,
        Methinks it should have power to steal both his,
        And leave itself unfurnish'd. Yet look how far
        The substance of my praise doth wrong this
        shadow
        In underprizing it, so far this shadow
        Doth limp behind the substance.

                                (III, ii, 114–129)

PORTIA AND BASSANIO

Bass.   Fair lady, by your leave;
        I come by note, to give and to receive.
        Like one of two contending in a prize,
        That thinks he hath done well in people's eyes,
        Hearing applause and universal shout,
        Giddy in spirit, still gazing in a doubt
        Whether those peals of praise be his or no;
        So, thrice-fair lady, stand I even so,
        As doubtful whether what I see be true,
        Until confirm'd, sign'd, ratified by you.
Por.   You see me, Lord Bassanio, where I stand,
        Such as I am. Though for myself alone
        I would not be ambitious in my wish
        To wish myself much better, yet for you
        I would be trebled twenty times myself,
        A thousand times more fair, ten thousand times
        more rich,
        That only to stand high in your account
        I might in virtues, beauties, livings, friends,
        Exceed account. But the full sum of me
        Is sum of something which, to term in gross,
        Is an unlesson'd girl, unschool'd, unpractis'd;
        Happy in this, she is not yet so old
        But she may learn; happier than this,
        She is not bred so dull but she can learn;
        Happiest of all is that her gentle spirit
        Commits itself to yours to be directed,

As from her lord, her governor, her king.
Myself and what is mine to you and yours
Is now converted. But now I was the lord
Of this fair mansion, master of my servants,
Queen o'er myself; and even now, but now,
This house, these servants, and this same myself,
Are yours—my lord's. I give them with this ring,
Which when you part from, lose, or give away,
Let it presage the ruin of your love,
And be my vantage to exclaim on you.

Bass. Madam, you have bereft me of all words;
Only my blood speaks to you in my veins;
And there is such confusion in my powers
As, after some oration fairly spoke
By a beloved prince, there doth appear
Among the buzzing pleased multitude,
Where every something, being blent together,
Turns to a wild of nothing, save of joy
Express'd and not express'd. But when this ring
Parts from this finger, then parts life from hence;
O, then be bold to say Bassanio's dead!

(III, ii, 139–186)

JESSICA AND LORENZO

Lor. The moon shines bright. In such a night as this,
When the sweet wind did gently kiss the trees,
And they did make no noise—in such a night,
Troilus methinks mounted the Troyan walls,
And sigh'd his soul toward the Grecian tents,
Where Cressid lay that night.

Jes. In such a night
Did Thisby fearfully o'ertrip the dew,
And saw the lion's shadow ere himself,
And ran dismayed away.

Lor. In such a night
Stood Dido with a willow in her hand
Upon the wild sea-banks, and waft her love
To come again to Carthage.

Jes. In such a night
Medea gathered the enchanted herbs
That did renew old Æson.

Lor. In such a night
Did Jessica steal from the wealthy Jew,
And with an unthrift love did run from Venice
As far as Belmont.

Jes. In such a night
Did young Lorenzo swear he lov'd her well,
Stealing her soul with many vows of faith,
And ne'er a true one.

Lor. In such a night

Did pretty Jessica, like a little shrew,
Slander her love, and he forgave it her.

Jes.   I would out-night you, did no body come;
But, hark, I hear the footing of a man.

(*V, i, 1–22*)

As You Like It

FERTILITY SONG

It was a lover and his lass,
   With a hey, and a ho, and a hey nonino,
That o'er the green corn-field did pass
   In the spring time, the only pretty ring time,
When birds do sing, hey ding a ding, ding,
Sweet lovers love the spring.

Between the acres of the rye,
   With a hey, and a ho, and a hey nonino,
These pretty country folks would lie,
   In the spring time, the only pretty ring time,
When birds do sing, hey ding a ding, ding,
Sweet lovers love the spring.

This carol they began that hour,
   With a hey, and a ho, and a hey nonino,
How that a life was but a flower,
   In the spring time, the only pretty ring time,
When birds do sing, hey ding a ding, ding,
Sweet lovers love the spring.

And therefore take the present time,
   With a hey, and a ho, and a hey nonino,
For love is crowned with the prime,
   In the spring time, the only pretty ring time,
When birds do sing, hey ding a ding, ding,
Sweet lovers love the spring.

(V, iii, 14–31)

SILVIUS AND PHEBE

Phe.   I would not be thy executioner;
I fly thee, for I would not injure thee.
Thou tell'st me there is murder in mine eye.
'Tis pretty, sure, and very probable,
That eyes, that are the frail'st and softest things,
Who shut their coward gates on atomies,
Should be call'd tyrants, butchers, murderers!
Now I do frown on thee with all my heart;
And if mine eyes can wound, now let them kill
thee.
Now counterfeit to swoon; why, now fall down;
Or, if thou canst not, O, for shame, for shame,
Lie not, to say mine eyes are murderers.
Now show the wound mine eye hath made in thee.
Scratch thee but with a pin, and there remains
Some scar of it; lean upon a rush,
The cicatrice and capable impressure
Thy palm some moment keeps; but now mine eyes,
Which I have darted at thee, hurt thee not;
Nor, I am sure, there is not force in eyes
That can do hurt.

Sil.   O dear Phebe,
If ever—as that ever may be near—
You meet in some fresh cheek the power of fancy,
Then shall you know the wounds invisible
That love's keen arrows make.

Phe. But till that time
Come not thou near me; and when that time comes,
Afflict me with thy mocks, pity me not;
As till that time, I shall not pity thee.

(*III, v, 8–34*)

Twelfth Night

THE DUKE

Duke. If music be the food of love, play on,
Give me excess of it, that, surfeiting,
The appetite may sicken and so die.
That strain again! It had a dying fall;
O, it came o'er my ear like the sweet sound
That breathes upon a bank of violets,
Stealing and giving odour! Enough, no more;
'Tis not so sweet now as it was before.
O spirit of love, how quick and fresh art thou!
That, notwithstanding thy capacity
Receiveth as the sea, nought enters there,
Of what validity and pitch soe'er,
But falls into abatement and low price
Even in a minute. So full of shapes is fancy,
That it alone is high fantastical.

(I, i, 1–15)

TWELFTH NIGHT

VIOLA

Vio.   If I did love you in my master's flame,
With such a suff'ring, such a deadly life,
In your denial I would find no sense;
I would not understand it.

Oli.   Why, what would you?

Vio.   Make me a willow cabin at your gate,
And call upon my soul within the house;
Write loyal cantons of contemned love
And sing them loud even in the dead of night;
Halloo your name to the reverberate hills,
And make the babbling gossip of the air
Cry out 'Olivia!' O, you should not rest
Between the elements of air and earth
But you should pity me!

(*I, v, 248–260*)

TWELFTH NIGHT

CLOWN'S SONG

O mistress mine, where are you roaming?
O, stay and hear; your true love's coming,
   That can sing both high and low.
   Trip no further, pretty sweeting;
   Journeys end in lovers meeting,
   Every wise man's son doth know.

What is love? 'Tis not hereafter;
Present mirth hath present laughter;
   What's to come is still unsure.
In delay there lies no plenty,
Then come kiss me, sweet and twenty;
   Youth's a stuff will not endure.

(II, iii, 38–51)

OLIVIA

Oli. O, what a deal of scorn looks beautiful
In the contempt and anger of his lip!
A murd'rous guilt shows not itself more soon
Than love that would seem hid: love's night is noon.
Cesario, by the roses of the spring,
By maidhood, honour, truth, and every thing,
I love thee so that, maugre all thy pride,
Nor wit nor reason can my passion hide.
Do not extort thy reasons from this clause,
For that I woo, thou therefore hast no cause;
But rather reason thus with reason fetter:
Love sought is good, but given unsought is better.

(III, i, 142–153)

Troilus and Cressida

Tro.   When I do tell thee there my hopes lie drown'd,
Reply not in how many fathoms deep
They lie indrench'd. I tell thee I am mad
In Cressid's love. Thou answer'st 'She is fair'—
Pourest in the open ulcer of my heart—
Her eyes, her hair, her cheek, her gait, her voice,
Handlest in thy discourse. O, that her hand,
In whose comparison all whites are ink
Writing their own reproach; to whose soft seizure
The cygnet's down is harsh, and spirit of sense
Hard as the palm of ploughman! This thou tell'st me,
As true thou tell'st me, when I say I love her;
But, saying thus, instead of oil and balm,
Thou lay'st in every gash that love hath given me
The knife that made it.

(*I, i, 47–62*)

Pan.	Have you seen my cousin?
Tro.	No, Pandarus. I stalk about her door

Pan. Have you seen my cousin?
Tro. No, Pandarus. I stalk about her door
Like a strange soul upon the Stygian banks
Staying for waftage. O, be thou my Charon,
And give me swift transportance to these fields
Where I may wallow in the lily beds
Propos'd for the deserver! O gentle Pandar,
From Cupid's shoulder pluck his painted wings,
And fly with me to Cressid!
Pan. Walk here i' th' orchard, I'll bring her straight.
(*Exit*)
Tro. I am giddy; expectation whirls me round.
Th' imaginary relish is so sweet
That it enchants my sense; what will it be
When that the wat'ry palate tastes indeed
Love's thrice-repured nectar? Death, I fear me;
Swooning destruction; or some joy too fine,
Too subtle-potent, tun'd too sharp in sweetness,
For the capacity of my ruder powers.
I fear it much; and I do fear besides
That I shall lose distinction in my joys;
As doth a battle, when they charge on heaps
The enemy flying.

(*III, ii, 6–28*)

Cres.   Boldness comes to me now and brings me heart.
           Prince Troilus, I have lov'd you night and day
           For many weary months.
Tro.   Why was my Cressid then so hard to win?
Cres.   Hard to seem won; but I was won, my lord,
           With the first glance that ever—pardon me.
           If I confess much, you will play the tyrant.
           I love you now; but till now not so much
           But I might master it. In faith, I lie;
           My thoughts were like unbridled children, grown
           Too headstrong for their mother. See, we fools!
           Why have I blabb'd? Who shall be true to us,
           When we are so unsecret to ourselves?
           But, though I lov'd you well, I woo'd you not;
           And yet, good faith, I wish'd myself a man,
           Or that we women had men's privilege
           Of speaking first. Sweet, bid me hold my tongue,
           For in this rapture I shall surely speak
           The thing I shall repent. See, see, your silence,
           Cunning in dumbness, from my weakness draws
           My very soul of counsel. Stop my mouth.
Tro.   And shall, albeit sweet music issues thence.
Cres.   My lord, I do beseech you, pardon me;
           'Twas not my purpose thus to beg a kiss.
           I am asham'd. O heavens! what have I done?
           For this time will I take my leave, my lord.
Tro.   Your leave, sweet Cressid!
Cres.   Pray you, content you.
Tro.   What offends you, lady?
Cres.   Sir, mine own company.
Tro.   You cannot shun yourself.

Cres.   Let me go and try.
        I have a kind of self resides with you;
        But an unkind self, that it self will leave
        To be another's fool. I would be gone.
        Where is my wit? I know not what I speak.
Tro.   Well know they what they speak that speak so
        wisely.
Cres.   Perchance, my lord, I show more craft than love;
        And fell so roundly to a large confession
        To angle for your thoughts; but you are
        wise—
        Or else you love not; for to be wise and love
        Exceeds man's might; that dwells with gods above.
Tro.   O that I thought it could be in a woman—
        As, if it can, I will presume in you—
        To feed for aye her lamp and flames of love;
        To keep her constancy in plight and youth,
        Outliving beauty's outward, with a mind
        That doth renew swifter than blood decays!
        Or that persuasion could but thus convince me
        That my integrity and truth to you
        Might be affronted with the match and weight
        Of such a winnowed purity in love.
        How were I then uplifted! but, alas,
        I am as true as truth's simplicity,
        And simpler than the infancy of truth.
Cres.   In that I'll war with you.
Tro.   O virtuous fight,
        When right with right wars who shall be most right!
        True swains in love shall in the world to come
        Approve their truth by Troilus, when their rhymes,

TROILUS AND CRESSIDA

Full of protest, of oath, and big compare,
Want similes, truth tir'd with iteration—
As true as steel, as plantage to the moon,
As sun to day, as turtle to her mate,
As iron to adamant, as earth to th' centre—
Yet, after all comparisons of truth,
As truth's authentic author to be cited,
'As true as Troilus' shall crown up the verse
And sanctify the numbers.

Cres.　Prophet may you be!
If I be false, or swerve a hair from truth,
When time is old and hath forgot itself,
When waterdrops have worn the stones of Troy,
And blind oblivion swallow'd cities up,
And mighty states characterless are grated
To dusty nothing—yet let memory
From false to false, among false maids in love,
Upbraid my falsehood when th' have said 'As false
As air, as water, wind, or sandy earth,
As fox to lamb, or wolf to heifer's calf,
Pard to the hind, or stepdame to her son'—
Yea, let them say, to stick the heart of falsehood,
'As false as Cressid'.

(III, ii, 110–192)

TROILUS AND CRESSIDA

Cres.   I have forgot my father;
         I know no touch of consanguinity,
         No kin, no love, no blood, no soul so near me
         As the sweet Troilus. O you gods divine,
         Make Cressid's name the very crown of falsehood,
         If ever she leave Troilus! Time, force, and death,
         Do to this body what extremes you can,
         But the strong base and building of my love
         Is as the very centre of the earth,
         Drawing all things to it. I'll go in and weep—
         Tear my bright hair, and scratch my praised cheeks,
         Crack my clear voice with sobs and break my heart,
         With sounding 'Troilus'. I will not go from Troy.

                                    (IV, ii, 95–108)

All's Well
that Ends Well

HELENA AND BERTRAM

Hel.   I am undone; there is no living, none,
If Bertram be away. 'Twere all one
That I should love a bright particular star
And think to wed it, he is so above me.
In his bright radiance and collateral light
Must I be comforted, not in his sphere.
Th' ambition in my love thus plagues itself:
The hind that would be mated by the lion
Must die for love. 'Twas pretty, though a plague,
To see him every hour; to sit and draw
His arched brows, his hawking eye, his curls,
In our heart's table—heart too capable
Of every line and trick of his sweet favour.
But now he's gone, and my idolatrous fancy
Must sanctify his relics.

(*I, i, 78–92*)

196

ALL'S WELL THAT ENDS WELL

HELENA AND BERTRAM

Hel. Poor lord! is't I
      That chase thee from thy country, and expose
      Those tender limbs of thine to the event
      Of the none-sparing war? And is it I
      That drive thee from the sportive court, where thou
      Wast shot at with fair eyes, to be the mark
      Of smoky muskets? O you leaden messengers,
      That ride upon the violent speed of fire,
      Fly with false aim; move the still-piecing air,
      That sings with piercing; do not touch my lord.
      Whoever shoots at him, I set him there;
      Whoever charges on his forward breast,
      I am the caitiff that do hold him to't;
      And though I kill him not, I am the cause
      His death was so effected. Better 'twere
      I met the ravin lion when he roar'd
      With sharp constraint of hunger; better 'twere
      That all the miseries which nature owes
      Were mine at once. No; come thou home, Rousillon,
      Whence honour but of danger wins a scar,
      As oft it loses all. I will be gone.
      My being here it is that holds thee hence.
      Shall I stay here to do't? No, no, although
      The air of paradise did fan the house,
      And angels offic'd all. I will be gone,
      That pitiful rumour may report my flight
      To consolate thine ear. Come, night; end, day.
      For with the dark, poor thief, I'll steal away.

                              (*III, ii, 101–128*)

Measure for Measure

MARIANA

Take, O, take those lips away,
    That so sweetly were forsworn;
And those eyes, the break of day,
    Lights that do mislead the morn;
But my kisses bring again, bring again;
Seals of love, but seal'd in vain, seal'd in vain.

(IV, i, 1–6)

Othello

OTHELLO AND DESDEMONA

Othello describes how he won Desdemona's love.

Oth.	And, till she come, as faithful as to heaven
	I do confess the vices of my blood,
	So justly to your grave ears I'll present
	How I did thrive in this fair lady's love,
	And she in mine.
Duke.	Say it, Othello.
Oth.	Her father lov'd me, oft invited me;
	Still question'd me the story of my life
	From year to year—the battles, sieges, fortunes,
	That I have pass'd.
	I ran it through, even from my boyish days
	To th' very moment that he bade me tell it;
	Wherein I spake of most disastrous chances,
	Of moving accidents by flood and field;
	Of hairbreadth scapes i' th' imminent deadly breach;
	Of being taken by the insolent foe
	And sold to slavery; of my redemption thence,
	And portance in my travel's history;
	Wherein of antres vast and deserts idle,
	Rough quarries, rocks, and hills whose heads
	touch heaven,
	It was my hint to speak—such was the process;
	And of the Cannibals that each other eat,
	The Anthropophagi, and men whose heads

Do grow beneath their shoulders. This to hear
Would Desdemona seriously incline;
But still the house affairs would draw her thence;
Which ever as she could with haste dispatch.
She'd come again, and with a greedy ear
Devour up my discourse. Which I observing,
Took once a pliant hour, and found good means
To draw from her a prayer of earnest heart
That I would all my pilgrimage dilate,
Whereof by parcels she had something heard,
But not intentively. I did consent,
And often did beguile her of her tears,
When I did speak of some distressful stroke
That my youth suffer'd. My story being done,
She gave me for my pains a world of sighs;
She swore, in faith, 'twas strange, 'twas passing
strange;
'Twas pitiful, 'twas wondrous pitiful.
She wish'd she had not heard it; yet she wish'd
That heaven had made her such a man. She
thank'd me;
And bade me, if I had a friend that lov'd her,
I should but teach him how to tell my story,
And that would woo her. Upon this hint I spake;
She lov'd me for the dangers I had pass'd;
And I lov'd her that she did pity them.

(I, iii, 122–168)

OTHELLO AND DESDEMONA

Oth. O my fair warrior!
Des. My dear Othello!
Oth. It gives me wonder great as my content
        To see you here before me. O my soul's joy!
        If after every tempest come such calms,
        May the winds blow till they have waken'd death,
        And let the labouring bark climb hills of seas
        Olympus-high and duck again as low
        As hell's from heaven. If it were now to die,
        'Twere now to be most happy; for I fear
        My soul hath her content so absolute
        That not another comfort like to this
        Succeeds in unknown fate.
Des. The heavens forbid
        But that our loves and comforts should increase
        Even as our days do grow!
Oth. Amen to that, sweet powers!
        I cannot speak enough of this content;
        It stops me here; it is too much of joy.
        And this, and this, the greatest discords be
                                        (*They kiss*)
        That e'er our hearts shall make!

                                        (*II, i, 180–197*)

OTHELLO AND DESDEMONA

Des.   What shall I do to win my lord again?
Good friend, go to him; for, by this light of heaven,
I know not how I lost him. Here I kneel.
If e'er my will did trespass 'gainst his love,
Either in discourse of thought or actual deed,
Or that mine eyes, mine ears, or any sense,
Delighted them in any other form,
Or that I do not yet, and ever did,
And ever will—though he do shake me off
To beggarly divorcement—love him dearly,
Comfort forswear me! Unkindness may do much;
And his unkindness may defeat my life,
But never taint my love.

(IV, ii, 150–162)

OTHELLO AND DESDEMONA

Othello murders Desdemona out of jealousy.

Oth. It is the cause, it is the cause, my soul—
Let me not name it to you, you chaste stars—
It is the cause. Yet I'll not shed her blood,
Nor scar that whiter skin of hers than snow,
And smooth as monumental alabaster.
Yet she must die, else she'll betray more men.
Put out the light, and then put out the light.
If I quench thee, thou flaming minister,
I can again thy former light restore,
Should I repent me; but once put out thy light,
Thou cunning'st pattern of excelling nature,
I know not where is that Promethean heat
That can thy light relume. When I have pluck'd thy rose,
I cannot give it vital growth again;
It needs must wither. I'll smell thee on the tree.
                    (*Kissing her.*)
O balmy breath, that dost almost persuade
Justice to break her sword! One more, one more.
Be thus when thou art dead, and I will kill thee,
And love thee after. One more, and that's the last:
So sweet was ne'er so fatal. I must weep,
But they are cruel tears. This sorrow's heavenly;
It strikes where it doth love. She wakes.

                    (*V, ii, 1–22*)

Antony and Cleopatra

The death of Antony.

Cleo. Noblest of men, woo't die?
Hast thou no care of me? Shall I abide
In this dull world, which in thy absence is
No better than a sty? O, see, my women,

> *(Antony dies.)*

The crown o' th' earth doth melt. My lord!
O, wither'd is the garland of the war,
The soldier's pole is fall'n! Young boys and girls
Are level now with men. The odds is gone,
And there is nothing left remarkable
Beneath the visiting moon.

. . .

No more but e'en a woman, and commanded
By such poor passion as the maid that milks
And does the meanest chares. It were for me
To throw my sceptre at the injurious gods;
To tell them that this world did equal theirs
Till they had stol'n our jewel. All's but nought;
Patience is sottish, and impatience does
Become a dog that's mad. Then is it sin
To rush into the secret house of death
Ere death dare come to us?
Ah, women, women, look,
Our lamp is spent, it's out!

> *(IV, xv, 59–84)*

ANTONY AND CLEOPATRA

Cleopatra eulogises the dead Antony to her maid, Dolabella.

Cleo.   His face was as the heav'ns, and therein stuck
         A sun and moon, which kept their course and lighted
         The little O, the earth.
Dol.   Most sovereign creature—
Cleo.   His legs bestrid the ocean; his rear'd arm
         Crested the world. His voice was propertied
         As all the tuned spheres, and that to friends;
         But when he meant to quail and shake the orb,
         He was as rattling thunder. For his bounty,
         There was no winter in't; an autumn 'twas
         That grew the more by reaping. His delights
         Were dolphin-like: they show'd his back above
         The element they liv'd in. In his livery
         Walk'd crowns and crownets; realms and islands were
         As plates dropp'd from his pocket.
Dol.   Cleopatra—
Cleo.   Think you there was or might be such a man
         As this I dreamt of?
Dol.   Gentle madam, no.
Cleo.   You lie, up to the hearing of the gods.
         But if there be nor ever were one such,
         It's past the size of dreaming. Nature wants stuff
         To vie strange forms with fancy; yet t' imagine
         An Antony were nature's piece 'gainst fancy,
         Condemning shadows quite.

(*V, ii, 79–100*)

Cymbeline

IMOGEN AND POSTHUMUS

Imogen describes her parting from Posthumus to his servant Pisanio.

Imo.   I would have broke mine eye-strings, crack'd them
but
To look upon him, till the diminution
Of space had pointed him sharp as my needle;
Nay, followed him till he had melted from
The smallness of a gnat to air, and then
Have turn'd mine eye and wept. But, good Pisanio,
When shall we hear from him?

Pis.   Be assur'd, madam,
With his next vantage.

Imo.   I did not take my leave of him, but had
Most pretty things to say. Ere I could tell him
How I would think on him at certain hours
Such thoughts and such; or I could make him swear
The shes of Italy should not betray
Mine interest and his honour; or have charg'd him,
At the sixth hour of morn, at noon, at midnight,
T' encounter me with orisons, for then
I am in heaven for him; or ere I could
Give him that parting kiss which I had set
Betwixt two charming words, comes in my father,
And like the tyrannous breathing of the north
Shakes all our buds from growing.

(*I, iv, 17–37*)

206

The Winter's Tale

PERDITA AND FLORIZEL

Flo.   What you do
Still betters what is done. When you speak, sweet,
I'd have you do it ever. When you sing,
I'd have you buy and sell so; so give alms;
Pray so; and, for the ord'ring your affairs,
To sing them too. When you do dance, I wish you
A wave o' th' sea, that you might ever do
Nothing but that; move still, still so,
And own no other function. Each your doing,
So singular in each particular,
Crowns what you are doing in the present deeds,
That all your acts are queens.

                                       (*IV, iv, 135–146*)

The Tempest

FERDINAND AND MIRANDA

Fer.   Admir'd Miranda!
Indeed the top of admiration; worth
What's dearest to the world! Full many a lady
I have ey'd with best regard; and many a time
Th' harmony of their tongues hath into bondage
Brought my too diligent ear; for several virtues
Have I lik'd several women, never any
With so full soul, but some defect in her
Did quarrel with the noblest grace she ow'd,
And put it to the foil; but you, O you,
So perfect and so peerless, are created
Of every creature's best!

Mira.   I do not know
One of my sex; no woman's face remember,
Save, from my glass, mine own; nor have I seen
More that I may call men than you, good friend,
And my dear father. How features are abroad,
I am skilless of; but, by my modesty,
The jewel in my dower, I would not wish
Any companion in the world but you;
Nor can imagination form a shape,
Besides yourself, to like of.

    . . . .

Fer.   Hear my soul speak:

THE TEMPEST

>   The very instant that I saw you, did
>   My heart fly to your service; there resides
>   To make me slave to it; and for your sake
>   Am I this patient log-man.
> *Mira.*   Do you love me?
> *Fer.*   O heaven, O earth, bear witness to this sound,
>   And crown what I profess with kind event,
>   If I speak true! If hollowly, invert
>   What best is boded me to mischief! I,
>   Beyond all limit of what else i' th' world,
>   Do love, prize, honour you.
> *Mira.*   I am a fool
>   To weep at what I am glad of.
> *Fer.*   Wherefore weep you?
> *Mira.*   At mine unworthiness, that dare not offer
>   What I desire to give, and much less take
>   What I shall die to want. But this is trifling;
>   And all the more it seeks to hide itself,
>   The bigger bulk it shows. Hence, bashful cunning!
>   And prompt me plain and holy innocence!
>   I am your wife, if you will marry me;
>   If not, I'll die your maid. To be your fellow
>   You may deny me; but I'll be your servant,
>   Whether you will or no.
> *Fer.*   My mistress, dearest;
>   And I thus humble ever.
> *Mira.*   My husband, then?
> *Fer.*   Ay, with a heart as willing
>   As bondage e'er of freedom. Here's my hand.
> Mira.   And mine, with my heart in't. And now farewell
>   Till half an hour hence.
> Fer.   A thousand thousand!

                                                      (*III, i, 37–91*)

The Two
Noble Kinsmen

---·---

AMELIA

Amelia describes her love for her sister, Flavina.

You talk of Pirithous' and Theseus' love:
Theirs has more ground, is more maturely season'd,
More buckled with strong judgment, and their needs
The one of th' other may be said to water
Their intertangled roots of love, but I
And she (I sigh and spoke of) were things innocent,
Lov'd for we did, and like the elements
That know not what nor why, yet do effect
Rare issues by their operance, our souls
Did so to one another. What she lik'd
Was then of me approv'd, what not, condemn'd,
No more arraignment. The flow'r that I would pluck
And put between my breasts (O then but beginning
To swell about the blossom), she would long
Till she had such another, and commit it
To the like innocent cradle, where phœnix-like
They died in perfume. On my head no toy
But was her pattern, her affections (pretty,
Though happily her careless wear) I followed
For my most serious decking. Had mine ear
Stol'n some new air, or at adventure humm'd one
From musical coinage, why, it was a note

Whereon her spirits would sojourn (rather dwell on)
And sing it in her slumbers. This rehearsal
(Which, ev'ry innocent wots well, comes in
Like old importment's bastard) has this end,
That the true love 'tween maid and maid may be
More than in sex dividual.

(I, iii, 55–82)

Venus and Adonis

'Fondling,' she saith 'since I have hemm'd thee here
Within the circuit of this ivory pale,
I'll be a park, and thou shalt be my deer;
Feed where thou wilt, on mountain or in dale;
Graze on my lips; and if those hills be dry,
Stray lower, where the pleasant fountains lie.

Within this limit is relief enough,
Sweet bottom-grass, and high delightful plain,
Round rising hillocks, brakes obscure and rough,
To shelter thee from tempest and from rain;
Then be my deer, since I am such a park;
No dog shall rouse thee, though a thousand bark.'

(*lines 229–240*)

VENUS AND ADONIS

Had I no eyes but ears, my ears would love
That inward beauty and invisible;
Or were I deaf, thy outward parts would move
Each part in me that were but sensible.
Though neither eyes nor ears, to hear nor see,
Yet should I be in love by touching thee.

Say that the sense of feeling were bereft me,
And that I could not see, nor hear, nor touch,
And nothing but the very smell were left me,
Yet would my love to thee be still as much;
For from the stillitory of thy face excelling
Comes breath perfum'd, that breedeth love by smelling.

But, O, what banquet wert thou to the taste,
Being nurse and feeder of the other four!
Would they not wish the feast might ever last,
And bid Suspicion double-lock the door,
Lest Jealousy, that sour unwelcome guest,
Should by his stealing in disturb the feast?

(lines 433–450)

VENUS AND ADONIS

Venus's prophecy on the death of Adonis.

Since thou art dead, lo, here I prophesy
Sorrow on love hereafter shall attend:
It shall be waited on with jealousy,
Find sweet beginning but unsavoury end,
Ne'er settled equally, but high or low,
That all love's pleasure shall not match his woe.

It shall be fickle, false, and full of fraud,
Bud and be blasted in a breathing while,
The bottom poison, and the top o'erstraw'd
With sweets that shall the truest sight beguile;
The strongest body shall it make most weak,
Strike the wise dumb, and teach the fool to speak.

It shall be sparing, and too full of riot,
Teaching decrepit age to tread the measures;
The staring ruffian shall it keep in quiet,
Pluck down the rich, enrich the poor with treasures;
It shall be raging mad, and silly mild,
Make the young old, the old become a child.

It shall suspect where is no cause of fear;
It shall not fear where it should most mistrust;
It shall be merciful, and too severe,
And most deceiving when it seems most just;
Perverse it shall be where it shows most toward,
Put fear to valour, courage to the coward.

VENUS AND ADONIS

It shall be cause of war and dire events,
And set dissension 'twixt the son and sire,
Subject and servile to all discontents,
As dry combustious matter is to fire.
Sith in his prime death doth my love destroy,
They that love best their loves shall not enjoy.

(lines 1135–1164)

The Phœnix
and Turtle

Let the bird of loudest lay,
On the sole Arabian tree,
Herald sad and trumpet be,
To whose sound chaste wings obey.

But thou shrieking harbinger,
Foul precurrer of the fiend,
Augur of the fever's end,
To this troop come thou not near.

From this session interdict
Every fowl of tyrant wing,
Save the eagle, feath'red king:
Keep the obsequy so strict.

Let the priest in surplice white,
That defunctive music can,
Be the death-divining swan,
Lest the requiem lack his right.

And thou treble-dated crow,
That thy sable gender mak'st
With the breath thou giv'st and tak'st
'Mongst our mourners shalt thou go.

Here the anthem doth commence:
Love and constancy is dead;
Phœnix and the turtle fled
In a mutual flame from hence.

THE PHŒNIX AND THE TURTLE

So they lov'd as love in twain
Had the essence but in one;
Two distincts, division none:
Number there in love was slain.

Hearts remote, yet not asunder;
Distance, and no space was seen
'Twixt this turtle and his queen;
But in them it were a wonder.

So between them love did shine
That the turtle saw his right
Flaming in the phœnix' sight:
Either was the other's mine.

Property was thus appalled,
That the self was not the same;
Single nature's double name
Neither two nor one was called.

Reason, in itself confounded,
Saw division grow together,
To themselves yet either neither,
Simple were so well compounded,

That it cried 'How true a twain
Seemeth this concordant one!
Love hath reason, reason none,
If what parts can so remain'.

Whereupon it made this threne
To the phœnix and the dove,
Co-supremes and stars of love,
As chorus to their tragic scene.

THE PHŒNIX AND TURTLE

THRENOS

Beauty, truth, and rarity,
Grace in all simplicity,
Here enclos'd in cinders lie.

Death is now the phœnix' nest;
And the turtle's loyal breast
To eternity doth rest,

Leaving no posterity—
'Twas not their infirmity,
It was married chastity.

Truth may seem, but cannot be;
Beauty brag, but 'tis not she:
Truth and beauty buried be.

To this urn let those repair
That are either true or fair;
For these dead birds sigh a prayer.